the
light
and the
shadow

That's a brilliant idea . . . but how could it possibly work in my organization?

How often do you think as you read a business book that if only you could ask the author a simple question you could transform you organization?

Capstone is creating a unique partnership between authors and readers, delivering for the first time in business book publishing a genuine after-sales service for book buyers. Simply visit Capstone's home page on

http://www.bookshop.co.uk/capstone/

to leave your question (with details of date and place of purchase of a copy of *The Light and the Shadow*) and the authors will try to answer it. We do not promise 24-hour turnaround. But that one question answered might just jump-start your company and your career. Capstone is more than a publisher. It is an electronic clearing-house for pioneering management thinking, putting the creators of new business ideas in touch with the people who use them.

the light
and the
shadow

How Breakthrough Innovation is Shaping European Business

Otto Kalthoff
Ikujiro Nonaka
Pedro Nueno

Roland Berger Foundation

CAPSTONE

First published 1997
Capstone Publishing Limited
Oxford Centre for Innovation
Mill Street
Oxford OX2 0JX
United Kingdom

British Library Cataloguing in Publication Data
A CIP catalogue record for this book is available from the British Library

ISBN 1 900961 17 2

Designed and typeset by Forewords, Oxford
Printed and bound by T.J. Press Ltd, Padstow, Cornwall

This book is printed on acid-free paper

Contributors

Otto Kalthoff is a senior partner at Roland Berger and Partner GmbH and Director of the Roland Berger Foundation. He specializes in strategic management consultancy.

Jean-Paul Larçon is Professor of Strategy at the Hautes Etudes Commerciales (HEC) of Paris. A former Dean of HEC, he is one of the founding fathers of the CEMS (Community of European Management Schools) and the co-ordinator of HEC's International Mangement specialisation.

Ronnie Lessem is Reader in International Management and Academic Director of the consortium-based MBA at City University Business School, London. His major areas of teaching and research are transcultural business and organizational learning and knowledge creation. He acts as a consultant to companies in Europe, southern Africa and the Middle East, and has written some twenty books on management, organization and business development. He is a director of Concord Clothing, his family business in Zimbabwe.

Klaus Macharzina is President of the University of Hohenheim and Professor of Business Administration at the University of Hohenheim, Stuttgart. He is Director of the Research Centre for Export and Technology Management and editor of *Management International Review*.

Raoul C. C. Nacamulli is Full Professor of Management and Organization at the University of Reggio, Calabria, and Professor of Industrial Relations at Bocconi University. He is the Director of CRORA, the Research Centre of Organizational Effectiveness at Bocconi University.

Ikujiro Nonaka is Founding Dean of the Graduate Schord of Knowledge Science at the Japan Advanced Institute of Science and Technology (JAIST), Hokuriko, and a Professor at the Institute of Innovation Research, Hitotsubashi University. He is the co-author of *The Knowledge Creating Company*, which was awarded the 1995 Best Book of the Year in Business and Management.

Pedro Nueno is Bertran Foundation Professor of Entrepreneurial Management at the Instituto de Estudios Superiores de la Empresa (IESE), Barcelona. He is the Chancellor of the International Academy of Management and is also a Member of the Board and Chairman of the China Europe International Business School (CFIBS), Shanghai.

Philip Rosenzweig is Professor of Strategy and Organization at IMD. Prior to joining IMD in 1997 he was Professor of Business Administration at Harvard Business School. His main interests are the strategic management of multinational corporations, human resource management in multinational corporations, and the relationship between culture and management.

Acknowledgements

The authors would like to thank the companies researched for their support in data collection and numerous discussions. As representatives for many others we would like to mention David Potter at Psion, Prof. Dr Berthold Leibinger at Trumpf, Dr Detlev Humsdiek at Bertelsmann, Javier Mongelos and Jesús Larranaga at Mondragón, and Rodrigo Edenique from Banco de Santander.

In the process of writing this book there have been two interrelated concepts which have strongly informed its contents, especially in connection with the cultural diversity of Europe. For these related concepts of the 'Global Businesssphere' (Lessem and Palsule, 1997) and the 'Cultural Compass' (Lessem and Altman, 1996) we would like to acknowledge our debt to our colleague Ronnie Lessem and his associates.

Special thanks are owed to the Roland Berger Foundation, which financed this research, and its trustees, who gave valuable input in various discussions.

Special thanks are also due to David Sharman for the effort he took in structuring and editing the book.

Roland Berger Foundation

The Roland Berger Foundation was founded in 1992 on the occasion of the 25th anniversary of Roland Berger & Partner International Management Consultants. Its goal is the promotion and support of science development in the area of national and international management.

The foundation is headed by a council and supported by a board of trustees consisting of 19 CEOs of leading European companies.

Contents

Executive Summary   xi

Introduction   1

1   Europe: A Tradition of Business and Innovation   3

2   Two Themes: Innovation from Diversity and the   11
    European Imperative
    Universality and Diversity   11
    The European Model   14
    The European Imperative   15

3   *The Light and the Shadow* Explained   19
    The Case Studies   20
    The Light and the Shadow   22

Part 1   Knowledge and Innovation   23

4   Truth, Goodness and Beauty: The Foundations of   25
    Knowledge
    Plato's Concept of Knowledge   25
    Sources of Knowledge   27
    The Resonance of Knowledge   28
    Modifiers of Knowledge: Time and Place   29

5   Vision and Breadth: The Nature of Innovation   31
    Types of Innovations   31
    Commercialization and the Process of Innovation   32
    Plato's Concepts Applied to Innovation   34
    Innovation and Time   36

6   Time Past, Time Future: The Imperative of Innovation   39

7   The Character of Successful Innovative Companies   43
    Introduction   43
    David and Goliath: Microsoft and IBM in the USA   44
    Focusing on Utility: Psion in the UK   49
    Pursuing Service, Truth and Egalitarianism: 54
      Kao and Sharp in Japan
    Rationality, Precision and Accuracy: Trumpf and   60
      Bertelsmann in Germany
    Leading the World: Michelin and Salomon in France   64
    Economic and Social Renewal: Mondragón and   69
      Banco de Santander in Spain
    Managing Diversity: Versace and Esaote in Italy   73

8   Capturing the Universal Principles of Innovation   79
    Information: The Explicit Use of Information   80
      Sharing Mechanisms
    Linked Basic Competencies   83
    Leadership: The Presence of a Founder or CEO   85
      with a Clear Vision of Innovation
    Commitment to Innovation   90
    Strategy: A Long-term Approach to Management   91
      and a Basis of Stability
    Regeneration: A Willingness to Start All Over Again 95
    Distance between Innovation and the Market   98
    Organization: The Use of Flat Organizational   100
      Structures and Teamwork
    Resources: The Allocation of Resources to Support Innovation   105
    Incentivization: A Reward Structure that Supports   106
      Innovative Behaviour
    Equifinality: Different Roads to a Common Destination 108

Part 2 Diversity   111

9   Shadows of the Pyrenees: Describing Diversity   113
    Introduction   113
    Similarity and Diversity   114
    The Two Fallacies   116
    Levels of Geographical Diversity   117
    Common Ground, Diverse Culture   118

10 The Reef, the Garden and the Forest: 121
    The Diversity of the Triad
    The American Context   122
    The Japanese Context   125

The European Context 128
Leadership from the Centre 132
Family Ownership 133
The Development of Individuals 134
Separation from the Market 136
Introversion 138

11 Trees in the Forest: The Diversity of Europe 139
Anglo-Saxon Regions: Personal Capitalism 141
Germanic Regions: Co-operative Capitalism 143
Latin Regions: Regional Capitalism 145
Scandinavia: Social Capitalism 147
The Local Level 149

12 Complexity and Opportunity: 153
Diversity as a Source of Innovation
The Cultural Compass 154
The Cultural Compass and Spheres of Innovation 156

13 Diversity Revisited 159

Part 3 Implications 163

14 Universal Principles, Diverse Environments, 165
Unique Companies
The Light and the Shadow 165
Business Individuation 166

15 Towards the Future 169
Willingness to Change 169
Knowledge 170
Vision 172
Creation, Orientation and Elaboration, Commercialization 173
Diversity and Differentiation 174
Seeing the Shadow 176
Leadership 176
Hierarchy 177
Elites 179
Wider Roles 181

Part 4 The Leadership of Innovation 183

16   Music, Conductor and Orchestra   185
      Introduction   185
      The Conductor and the Orchestra: Links Between   187
         Innovation and Leadership
      Innovation, Leadership and Corporate Life Cycles   190
      Typology of Innovation-oriented Leadership Styles   194
      Ethical Leadership   206
      Conclusions   207

Epilogue   209

Bibliography   213

Index   219

Executive Summary

- -

There has been much recent focus within the business world on concepts such as restructuring, down-sizing, re-engineering and more. These concepts have their value, but they are inherently negative and inward-looking. Companies that want to succeed in the long term must look forwards and outwards towards growth and new opportunities. Innovation is the key to the future.

Innovation is often seen as the introduction of new products, and the responsibility of a few staff. But it is something much richer and more complex than this, and affects and is affected by many people across a company. It is exciting and creative, building on diverse knowledge and vision. In this book we examine successful innovative companies and from them capture the core principles of innovation.

Can these core principles be applied to all companies? The cultural diversity of different companies argues against this. We explore the subtlety of diversity and how companies need to respect their cultural heritage, particularly in Europe.

This leads us beyond the exploration of innovation and diversity to the second purpose of this book. Europe has a great tradition of innovation in the arts and sciences. It has also had a leading role in business innovation, but is now losing its way when contrasted against America or Japan. We believe that too many European companies have fallen into the mistake suggested in the previous paragraph and ignored their cultural heritage, applying inappropriate 'global' principles. But further beyond this still, Europe has lost its passion for innovation and its willingness to change and to challenge the future.

Europe must recapture its passion of innovation, sensitivity to culture and willingness to change. The style of this book will stimulate thought, not proscribe solutions, and we believe is fitting to these objectives.

Introduction

Chapter 1

- -

Europe: A Tradition of
Business and Innovation

The European quest for knowledge began in ancient Athens in the age of Socrates. It was Socrates who first steered the course of human enquiry towards things of the physical world rather than the gods and supernatural phenomena; it was the student of Socrates, Plato, who first elaborated a set of ideals by which humanity could live, fundamental goals towards which people could reach through art, science and design. Thus began the process by which innovation became part of the essence of European culture. Today, 2400 years later, innovation is bred into European bones, hardwired into the consciousness of the continent's intellectual elite. The quest for the new in every field, including philosophy and human sciences as well as mechanical science, is one of Europe's core themes; indeed, the three often go hand in hand.

Truth, goodness and beauty were the three ideals which Plato viewed as being the goals of a just society. The pursuit of these fundamentals has occupied European innovators in every sphere of thought and action ever since. In order to pursue these ideals, however, people require knowledge; faith and belief, while they can be important influences, are not requisite. It is knowledge, as we shall see later, that provides the fuel for innovation and determines its shape. Plato also believed that knowledge had many diverse shapes and natures: different modes of thought have different dominant forms of knowledge,

3

and so variety conspires to make up the whole of under-standing.

Plato himself failed to see his ideas put into effect: his one experiment in turning his own philosophy into practice and creating a true republic based on truth, goodness and beauty was a failure, and towards the end of his life he fell back on writing primarily about the nature of justice. The influence of his ideas, however, has been felt around the world. From the Platonic definitions of ideals and knowledge come the bases of the modern physical and psychological sciences. For the next millennia and a half, western (and Middle Eastern) philosophy and science took Plato and his pupil Aristotle as their direct inspiration; in the middle ages, his works resurfaced as the inspiration behind a new movement of enquiry known as scholasticism, which in turn touched off the modern scientific revolution that propelled Europe to four centuries of world leadership.

By the year 1107 AD, Paris had become famous as the European centre of learning. It was in that year that an ambitious young scholar and theologian named Peter Abelard first made his mark, by publicly debating with and destroying the reputation of a respected orthodox scholar, William of Champeaux. Abelard was unique in many respects. First, unlike most scholars of the day, he was not a priest or a monk but a layman, the son of a knight. Second, he held scant regard for the prevailing philosophical and religious positions, many of which had been handed down from the early Christian period and which relied on faith rather than reason. Reason, however, was Abelard's kingdom; from within its boundaries he attacked the sacred cows of his day. His personal misfortunes (after embarking on a passionate affair with one of his female pupils, he was castrated by the pupil's vengeful uncle) seem only to have stimulated his desire for intellectual combat.

Challenge and argument were part of Abelard's make-up. Whereas conventional wisdom agreed with St Anselm, whose view that *credo ergo cognito* ('I believe, therefore I know') summed up the prevailing view that faith alone was enough to sustain people, Abelard challenged this wisdom with his famous doctrine: 'By doubting we come to examine, and by examining so we perceive the truth'. No aspect of philosophy was immune to his probing inquisitions. Repeatedly condemned by the Catholic Church, Abelard nonetheless set the pace for philosophical enquiry over the centuries that followed, and created the climate for intellectual enquiry that led to the scientific discoveries of Descartes and Newton five centuries later.

This spirit is still present in European culture today. From Abelard's time on, the pace of enquiry, discovery and innovation has rarely faltered. Curiosity and enquiry have become embedded in European culture. Philosophical enquiry has led in turn to curiosity about the physical world, the need for knowledge of humans as individuals and the need for understanding of the interaction of groups, and the desire for technological progress. Driving all of these have been the three Platonic concepts of truth, goodness and beauty; the higher things towards European civilization has always striven.

In the spring of 1434, Prince Henry of Portugal stood on a headland near the town of Sagres in Southwest Portugal, watching a ship disappear over the horizon. The ship, a small caravel captained by the navigator Gil Eannes, had a simple mission; to find a route around Cape Bojador on the Moroccan coast south of the Canary Islands, then marking the southern limit of exploration. For Prince Henry, known to history as Henry the Navigator, this marked the beginning of a personal campaign in search of truth, goodness and beauty by exploring the limits of the known world; for the world, it marked the beginning of the period of European discovery and colonialism.

The rate of progress of this revolution was phenomenal. By 1460, the year of Prince Henry's death, Portuguese ships had reached Sierra Leone, and by this time the momentum he had begun was strong enough to survive him. In 1488 Bartolomeu Dias rounded the Cape of Good Hope and reached the southern tip of Africa; in 1498 Vasco da Gama dropped anchor off the

Indian port of Calicut; in 1509 the Portuguese conquered the city of Malacca in modern Malaysia, and in 1513 – just seventy years after Gil Eannes set out for Cape Bojador – Portuguese ships arrived at Canton in southern China. The road to Cathay, a European dream for centuries, had been opened in less than a lifetime, all with tiny wooden ships with canvas sails and crude navigational instruments. From being an expanse of unknown, the world quickly became a vast frontier where men routinely ventured forth on voyages of exploration and trade; from the closed world of the early middle ages where people feared what lay beyond the bounds of the known world, we reach in less than a century the confidence of the English writer who declared: 'There is no land uninhabitable or sea innavigable.'

Prince Henry's voyages of discovery were also voyages of trade, and world trade became for a time the new frontier of discovery and imagination. Even in the Far East, Portuguese and Spanish traders served as middlemen between mutually antagonistic Japan and China. Europe grew rich off this trade, and the wealth provided was invested in the economy in a variety of forms. As economies grew they became more complex, and this led in turn to further increases in wealth. In 1776, the 53-year-old Scottish academic and economist Adam Smith, observing this activity, wrote:

> The rich only select from the heap what is most precious and agreeable. They consume little more than the poor. . . . They are led by an invisible hand to make nearly the same distribution of the necessaries of life which would have been made, had the earth been divided into equal portions among all its inhabitants, and thus without intending it, without knowing it, advance the interests of society and afford means to its multiplication.

Smith was not so much an innovator himself as a catalyst for thought and development. He synthesized a previously unorganized and divided field and made it into a discipline;

more, he provided ideas on economic factors in such a way as to make them easily accessible and therefore more open to debate. From Smith we have theories of value and definitions of the three factors of production, land, labour and capital, which have continued to provide a foundation for economic theory down to today; writers on economics as diverse as Lenin and Hayek have acknowledged their debt to him. *The Wealth of Nations* marks the beginning of our understanding in a scientific sense of the fundamental forces of economics, the 'invisible hand' which affects all our lives. His influence was further strengthened by his relating the ideas of economics to the moral dimension of human action.

The discipline of economics, which Smith did so much to found, has produced many notable European thinkers. One of the foremost is Max Weber, who began his career as a professor of economics at Heidelberg in 1896. Shortly thereafter he was forced to retire after having suffered a nervous breakdown and, while convalescing, wrote his most famous work, *The Protestant Ethic and the Spirit of Capitalism*, first published in 1905. His illness may have been a factor in his interest in rationalism – John Stewart Mill is another economist who suffered from nervous illness and exhibited a strong rationalist tendency – and it is his theories on rationalism that continue to have an effect on historians, economies and businesses alike.

Among the greatest of all European innovations is that of the corporation. The prototypes of the twentieth century international corporation were established in northern Italy around the time of the First Crusade (1096-99). They had their origins in the high-value, high-risk trades in eastern goods between western Europe and Asia, particularly spices and industrial goods such as alum, important in medicines and in cloth-making. Companies were founded as societies of traders banding together to invest capital, take advantage of economies of scale and share risk, given the high costs of shipping goods by land and sea over very long distances.

Though primitive by modern standards, these early companies were sophisticated operations, and the Zaccaria

Company and the Bank of St George, names forgotten now by all but a few historians, were the ancestors of today's multinationals. By 1300, they and others like them were selling shares and every major centre had its bourse, or stock exchange; governments and private companies had also begun selling bonds. Double-entry bookkeeping, the foundation of modern accounting, had been established as standard practice; schools, the forerunners of modern business schools, had been established to teach accounting and other standard business practices. Banking had become increasingly sophisticated with the introduction of notes of exchange and European-wide systems of credit and lending; when the English government defaulted on its loans in the mid-fourteenth century, it was Italian banks which suffered. Maritime insurance was also developing into a free-standing market. As companies grew in size and established overseas operations they used a variety of growth strategies, including direct ownership, agency and early forms of franchising. Businesses had become truly international; one Genoese firm had agents working simultaneously in China and Iceland, and large operations in every major western European country.

The techniques of trade spread quickly to manufacturing. In the cloth trade, which had roughly the same economic significance in western Europe that oil or electronics have in the late twentieth century, entrepreneurs began by farming out tasks such as weaving and dyeing to sub-contractors but quickly learned the benefits of concentrating production in house; thus were born the great cloth industries of north Italy, whose techniques quickly spread to Flanders and then to north Germany and England. Here we see the beginnings of the divergence of European models of business between the Latin, the Germanic and the Anglo-Saxon. In Italy and the south, where feudalism was weak or non-existing, large businesses were built on inter-related networks of families, the Medici of Florence being the most famous example. In Germany, feudalism was stronger and authoritarianism was a more important characteristic; locality and community became more important in, for example, the states of the Hanseatic League, than family. In England, where by 1350 the middle classes had achieved an early parity with the relatively weak nobility, dominant individuals came to the fore.

As time passed, businesses evolved and became still more complex. New markets opened up around the world, while political and economic changes caused shifts in relative economic power. The centre of banking moved from Florence in the fifteenth century to Genoa in the sixteenth, to Antwerp in the seventeenth and then to London in the eighteenth. Economics emerged as a discipline in its own right in 1776 with the publication of Adam Smith's *The Wealth of Nations*.

By the beginning of the twentieth century, business European-style dominated the globe; it had served as the source of business in the United States, whose then dominant population were themselves European immigrants; it had, through the US and directly, served as the model for the Japanese economic transformation under the Emperor Meiji and for the emerging foreign trading houses of China and southeast Asia. Other societies and civilization conducted trade and commerce, but none on the scale or sophistication of Europe; and when Europe opened up the globe in the late fifteenth century and beyond, the European model of business quickly swamped local systems. It is possible to argue that modern *business* – as distinct from *management* – has been moulded more by Europe than anyone else.

From these examples – and there are others – it can be seen that Europe has a strong tradition in both innovation and business. The histories of both European innovation and European business have not always been pleasant; they have seen exploitation, colonialism, slavery, the turning of technology to evil uses by dictators. But they have also seen the human spirit rise to challenge after challenge, to make breakthrough after breakthrough, to elevate the European standard of living to levels undreamed of by our ancestors.

Chapter 2

Two Themes: Innovation from Diversity and the European Imperative

Universality and Diversity

The challenge of diversity is to turn away from the light, towards the shadow of the unknown which lies outside the firm. The shadow has many elements. It includes other firms (competitors and otherwise), consumers, suppliers and all the traditional stakeholders in the firm; importantly, it also includes more distant influences such as culture, religion and environment. In understanding diversity, firms and managers need to confront those things which lie beyond their reach.

As this book demonstrates, many universal principles are valid; indeed, the research on which the book is based confirmed many of these principles, which are described in full in Chapter 7. At the same time, however, these universals can and should be harmonized with the many possibilities opened up by the recognition of diversity. By combining universal aspects of good management with factors occasioned by the firm's own cultural heritage and environment – and indeed by carefully mixing and matching appropriate factors borrowed from other environments – firms can create their own unique platform for innovation. From this uniqueness, competitive advantage can be developed. In contrast, ignoring a firm's heritage will cripple the effectiveness of the universal principles.

A platform for innovation built on foundations of diversity has greater potential than one built on undifferentiated foundations. As the book will describe, it is diversity of knowledge and vision which allows the greatest heights of innovation to be reached. Thus, although diversity may be perceived sometimes as a roadblock to innovation, it ultimately turns out to provide additional opportunities.

The attractiveness of the universal approach, the 'one best way', lies in part in its simplicity. As McLuhan (1964: 5) has observed, 'Every culture and every age has its favourite model of perception and knowledge that it is inclined to prescribe for everybody and everything.' Universal models are attractive because they are simple, powerful (sometimes deceptively so) and easy to understand. In business, the essence of management is often boiled down to a few basic principles which are often summarized by mnemonics or buzzwords. Easily memorized and understood, these concepts, when properly exploited, are sound. Too often, however, they are clung to like a lifeline in the face of circumstances which would seem to indicate that deviance from established 'rules' is required. Managing diversity is more difficult. It requires greater flexibility, a willingness to fly in the face of established beliefs about organization and management, a greater under-standing of the interaction of firms with their environment on all levels, not just that of the market, and a willingness to accept that other models of belief and behaviour can be just as valid as one's own.

The second attractive feature of the universalist approach is that it focuses on the (at least theoretically) known, the firm itself and its structures and processes. The managerial revolution of the mid-twentieth century has been described vividly by Chandler as the emergence of the 'visible hand' guiding businesses, as opposed to the 'invisible hand' which he (following Adam Smith) defined as the mechanisms of the market (Chandler 1977). Before him, Drucker had defined the manager as playing a pivotal role in the company; without the manager, Drucker argued, there could be no company. The universalist approach searches for 'one best way' in which managers can organize their companies to produce the maximum results. The universal values by which all companies abide – leadership, investment, structure, training, information, reward systems – are things which all managers (again, at least in theory) can identify in their own firms. Indeed, the spotlight has been on these factors for so long that many managers are in danger of being blinded. Market and environmental challenges are met almost instinctively with internal responses; loss of a traditional market is met with downsizing and delayering, control problems are responded to with investments in information technology, often without regard to whether these responses are truly appropriate.

The third attraction of the universalist approach is its seeming applicability to the domestic markets of the United States and Japan, where business cultures are relatively homogeneous within their own borders; harmonized systems would seem to be logically possible in a culture where firm behaviours and goals are roughly similar.

However, despite its attractions, the 'one best way' is an imperfect approach. And, in an increasingly globalized marketplace, it is the heterogeneity exemplified by Europe which provides a more appropriate metaphor for global business. The potential for European firms to cope effectively with different cultural, legal, societal and linguistic environments is an asset that can in turn be successfully invested in the international business environment. In this perspective, Europe can be seen as a laboratory for nourishing global management, and perhaps has some lessons for the multi-national, multi-cultural companies which have their roots more in the American or Japanese tradition.

The European Model

The need to accept and build upon diversity flies in the face of much conventional wisdom. Current – and past – trends in management thinking tend to focus on universal principles. From scientific management, which laid down rules by which processes could be carried out in the most economically efficient manner, to re-engineering, which at least has the virtue of trying to combine efficiency with effectiveness, management thinkers and practitioners have groped for a 'one best way', an ultimate model of the company and management which would ensure or at least improve the chances of success. Throughout much of the twentieth century, the ultimate model was seen in the American corporation, itself the source of the powerful economic growth that made the USA the wealthiest nation in the world. Later, as American prosperity began to look less secure, attention transferred to the Japanese model. Japanese corporations had in only a few decades lifted their country and economy from the ruins following the Second World War to the heights of global economic power, a transformation which seemed almost miraculous to American companies forced to struggle against Japanese competition, and for many the Japanese model became seen as the new 'one best way'.

In this search, Europe has largely been ignored. Although attempts have been made to synthesize European business culture (e.g. Whitley, 1993; Calori and de Woot, 1994), these attempts inevitably have to face the challenge of diversity: Europe is characterized more by heterogeneity than homogeneity. There are many ways, many forms of companies and businesses; there is no discernible 'one best way'. European diversity defies the attempts of theorists to find a single model for success. As a result, when management gurus over the last two decades set out to compile their lists of model companies, very few European companies are included; their individuality seems to rule them out of contention for managers seeking a model to copy.

The European paradox exposes the limitations of the

'one best way' approach, particularly where innovation is concerned. Innovation is strongly influenced by culture; local, national and regional attitudes to creativity, work and discipline play a crucial role in determining both the source and form of innovative behaviour. The fact that very innovative companies have appeared in many different parts of Europe, and in a variety of forms ranging from traditional hierarchies to grouped cooperatives, must surely expose the fact that innovation can come from many sources and be exploited in many ways. There is not one model for success; rather, there are many. For managers and companies seeking to develop and exploit innovation, there is a rich and sometimes dazzling diversity of structures and techniques from which to choose.

The European lesson is that for every certainty there is also an uncertainty. When managers in different cultures across Europe believe that their culture is 'the best', then there is the potential for conflict. But increasingly, as they work in close proximity to one another, European managers and firms are learning to learn from one another, while at the same time not giving up their own identities and strengths. Similarly, as the world grows smaller and global markets expand, European companies find themselves growing closer to their American and Japanese counterparts and rivals. These companies too, in many ways very different yet in many ways alike, offer sources of learning and understanding, while at the same time European business culture still has many lessons to teach the rest of the world.

The European Imperative

The last few years have seen European (and other) companies attempt to become more efficient by cutting back on labour costs and reducing personnel numbers. One standard measure, the number of employees in the national workforce per million dollars GDP, has declined dramatically. In Germany in the quarter century from 1970 to 1995 the number fell from 29 to

17, in France from 30 to 18, in Britain from 40 to 25 and, most dramatically, in Spain from 48 to 23. Although it is true that with fewer employees those employees who remain are individually now more productive, the efficiency gains from this reduction are now all but exhausted, especially in Germany and France. Further cutbacks will result not in cutting to the bone, but through it.

Even more worrying is the European position with regard to R&D. Overall European expenditure in this field remains high but, thanks to lack of international co-operation and lack of public-private sector co-operation, there is considerable redundancy of effort; in Japan and the United States, these redundancies are far fewer. Similarly, there are still large numbers of patents being registered in Europe every year, but an increasing proportion of these are being registered by non-European companies; the number of European patents registered abroad is falling. Britain, for example, still has a strong balance of payments surplus in technology invisibles to the newly-industrializing economies of east Asia, but its surplus with Japan is negligible, and its position with regard to America is one of deficit. From 1870 to 1920, America's industrial growth was fuelled by elaboration on European scientific progress; from 1950 until very recently, the Japanese industrial renaissance was propelled by elaboration on both European and American discoveries. Only in the last decade has Japanese R&D expenditure begun to outstrip that of Europe and America. Today, European companies are faced with competitors in Asia and America who are at least as techno- logically sophisticated and very often superior in terms of translating innovations into marketable products and services. Not only the profitability of European companies but the prosperity of Europe as a whole depend on the ability of firms and governments to reverse this situation.

Yet, a century ago, it was British and European science, British and European technology that fuelled the American industrial boom. What has happened? Why have we lost our way? Two major wars have, it is true, sapped European vitality to some extent; but the last of these conflicts is now fifty years old, and even the countries most damaged by them have enjoyed uninterrupted growth ever since. Various other explanations have been offered; the followers of Hayek and Friedman blame socialism and state interference in the economy, but another school, pointing to the economic successes of East Asia, argues that more rather than less state intervention is needed.

The heart of the problem seems to be that, for whatever reason, we have forgotten our heritage of innovation, vision and creativity. We have allowed ourselves to be persuaded that our ways of doing business – hierarchical, elitist, rooted in tradition and embedded in culture – are wrong, and that the democratic Americans and/or the communally-oriented Japanese firms represent the one true model of management. Small wonder, perhaps, that the innovation light is failing.

Chapter 3

- -

The Light and the Shadow **Explained**

The book's style is descriptive, not prescriptive. Its purpose is to examine cultures of innovation and success factors, with specific reference to the diverse cultures of Europe in comparison with those of the United States and Japan. It does not attempt to provide a path to innovation suitable for each diverse company. What is does intend to do is to stimulate thought and to provide a framework for analysis with which a manager can construct a solution unique to his or her own environment. It has to be read with an open and creative mind and has to be applied, not simply copied. This task of the reader is in itself a metaphor for innovation: it is the application of knowledge.

The book itself is the outgrowth of a collective process. The overarching metaphor is that of the title, the light and the shadow. The key word here is *and*. Light and shadow are not opposites; they are two halves of the same thing. Perhaps it is here that Europe and America have the most to learn from Asia, where 'and' thinking is more of a norm. In any case, this book could not have been written without 'and' thinking. During the planning stages of this book, eight contributors from seven countries brought their own often diverse ideas and arguments to the table. The book you hold in your hands represents the results not of a competition, where 'good' ideas 'won' over 'bad' ones, but of a collaboration, a process of synthesis whereby the ideas of all eight became linked as part of a much larger vision. This process itself could almost be seen as a metaphor for multi-cultural innovation; collective yet independent, harmonious yet competitive, original yet conscious of tradition.

The Case Studies

In order to explore innovation, we conducted a study of thirteen firms which we had previously identified as being particularly successful innovators. This was the most important common characteristic; otherwise the firms chosen were widely varied in terms of geography, firm history and background, size and industrial segment. All three major industrialized regions – Japan, North America and Europe – are represented; within Europe, the study encompasses five nations, France, Germany, the UK, Italy and Spain. The firms are also from a wide variety of industries, including tires (Michelin), ski boots and sporting goods (Salomon), hand-held computers and scientific instruments (Psion), biomedical instruments (Esaote), fashion (Versace), banking (Santander), a diversified co-operative (Mondragón), publishing and media (Bertlesmann), machine tools (Trumpf), consumer products (Kao), electronics (Sharp), software (Microsoft) and computers (IBM). The size range includes firms as large as IBM and as small as Psion. In terms of background, family-owned firms, public corporations, recent start-ups and firms with long histories were all included.

This is a qualitative study only, and there has been no attempt at statistical analysis. This is a study of exploration and description. As one of the primary goals was the study of diversity, it was important that the firms should reflect a variety of backgrounds; it was important too that they should reflect the backgrounds of the researchers, themselves a highly varied and heterogeneous group from seven different country backgrounds (Germany, France, Italy, Spain, the UK, Japan and the United States). As noted, the one common feature was that all thirteen companies were strongly innovative in some way or combination of ways, and were in a roughly similar situation in terms of innovation at the time the studies took place.

Nor should the study be regarded as all-inclusive. There are innovative firms in other regions of the world – notably east Asia outside Japan – which could have been studied, and even within Europe two important regions have been omitted. The first is Scandinavia, which has a distinctive culture of its own; we will make reference to Scandinavian companies and culture as we go along. The second is central and eastern Europe, where recent research (EFER, 1995) has shown that a number of interesting innovations are now occurring, particularly in countries such as the Czech Republic which are beginning in the post-Iron Curtain period to rediscover their own entrepreneurial heritage. In the 1920s and 1930s, entrepreneurs such as Tomas Bata developed a distinct East European model of management, and it is possible that such a model may emerge again. There also may well be – indeed, almost certainly are – other companies within the chosen regions or cultures which better exemplify innovation. We acknowledge this, but it is not the point. The aim of this book is to describe diversity in a European context; the thirteen case studies are chosen as exemplars, not as attempts to describe the whole situation.

A key aspect of the study, however, is the inclusion of benchmarks from among US and Japanese companies. It is pointless to even attempt to study European business culture in isolation, not when American and Japanese firms (including the four described here) are trading in Europe and when the European firms described here are themselves trading in world markets. Just as it is impossible to look clearly at German or Italian firms without describing their other European counterparts, so too it is impossible to get a true picture of European business culture without also looking at other similar cultures around the world. Thus, although this book is primarily about innovation in Europe, it is recognized from the outset that Europe does not exist in isolation and the European innovation can only properly be understood in a global context.

The Light and the Shadow

Thus we look out from the light places where we stand and see into the shadow. And thus it is – and this is the crucial point of the metaphor of light and shadow – that by learning, we recognize what the shadow is, and by recognizing it, learn more about the light. The process is simple: know yourself before you can know others; know others before you can know yourself. This applies to organizations as much as individuals, and in a world where knowledge is perhaps the most critical resource of all, the concept is more applicable still.

Part I

Knowledge and Innovation

Chapter 4

Truth, Goodness and Beauty: The Foundations of Knowledge

Plato's Concept of Knowledge

Knowledge, combined with vision, leads to innovation. In our journey through the spheres of innovation we need to start from a firm understanding of what these concepts mean and how they are related. Fortunately, in the European tradition we have a metaphor close to hand which will aid that understanding. That metaphor is Plato's concept of *truth*, *goodness* and *beauty*.

Plato was the first European to try to reconcile all the various aspects of knowledge, learned and inherited, logical and intuitive. In his conceptualization, 'beauty' is something we see intuitively; we know a thing is beautiful without the application of logic, and it is our understanding of beauty that leads us to intuitive judgement. There is a universal standard of beauty which can be defined, but each of us has our own appreciation of it. For example, two people are watching the same sunset; one will be moved by the colours of the light in the sky, while the other may be entranced by the movement of shadows as darkness falls. Beauty is in the mind, rather than the eye, of the beholder.

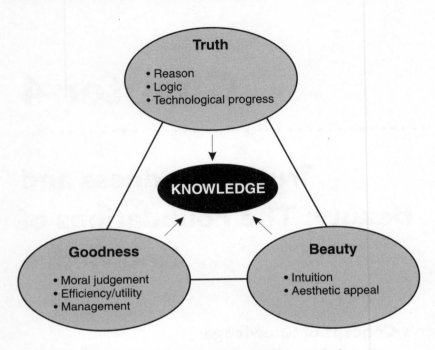

Figure 4.1 The foundations of knowledge

Goodness represents a different order of knowledge. Here, moral judgements come into play; we begin to examine whether a thing might be 'better' than another thing. These judgements are subjective but, provided we realize this and provided we make them within the generally accepted frameworks provided by society, there is no harm in this. Judgements of goodness can, for example focus on issues of efficiency and utility as well as value and profit.

Truth, the third order, represents the processes of reason in contrast to beauty's intuition. Truth, says Plato, can be arrived at logically; indeed it must be, or there is a danger that it will not be truth. However, he does not see truth and beauty as opposites. Human nature is such, he believes, that that which we intuitively perceive as beautiful must logically be true, while that which is true must also possess aesthetic qualities of beauty. If we do not see these things, or if we see them falsely, then it is because we lack the knowledge to do so.

These are fundamentals of knowledge, and they have been passed down through European philosophy, art, science and education for centuries. Beauty, goodness and truth are ideals with which most Europeans are familiar. Other cultures may have other ideals: on a more concrete level, freedom, for example, might be an American ideal, and harmony might be an Asian ideal, although it can argued that there are strong links between these and our European ideals (harmony partakes of truth and beauty, freedom of truth and goodness). For Europeans, these things are part of their psychological and social inheritance; their religions, cultures and learning have been shaped in these three moulds.

Sources of Knowledge

Knowledge can be newly created – within the concept of this book we will think of this as the act of invention, or knowledge can already exist and simply be made available. This simple difference has deep implications in the way knowledge is viewed within different cultures, and the way in which companies can manage knowledge.

Creating new knowledge often requires individuals to be given the freedom and motivation to indulge in the creative act, distanced from the usual corporate structures. In contrast, accessing existing knowledge requires co-operating groups with supporting information systems. Perhaps more important than these organisational and process concerns are the cultural attitudes towards knowledge. American society has a belief in the value of the new, including new knowledge, and is ready to invent. Japanese society has a long tradition, in art as well as business, that to copy and improve upon good work is an honourable and worth achievement. European society, during the Renaissance, had the same beliefs but these were slowly replaced by the nowadays more American attitudes applauding unique original and individual thought.

Considering in particular the use of existing knowledge as

a source upon which innovation can be built leads us to the multi-level character of knowledge and innovation, which is closely bound up with notions of synergy, interdependence and interactive organizational learning. A firm's capacity to innovate is not simply the sum of individual capabilities; rather, it is the result of an intricate interplay at numerous levels, individual, structural and societal (Van de Ven, 1986; Kanter, 1988; Frost and Egri, 1991). Yoshio Maruta, former president of Kao, puts it this way:

> The wisdom of a corporation . . . is the amassed knowledge of all members. Of course, all members of the board including the president must exert the utmost effort to form this corporate intelligence. But they have to be aware that they are only a part of the whole. A big corporation is separated into many sections. If that organization does not have the system to integrate the knowledge of each section, it cannot create any high-quality knowledge. Each section's knowledge must not only be the knowledge of its head but the combined knowledge of all members.

The Resonance of Knowledge

A single piece of knowledge, left in isolation, is usually of little value. Likewise many pieces of knowledge, without relationships, are of little value. Knowledge becomes of value when ideas can be related, and a set of ideas, in carefully related areas, can resonate with each other to produce an explosion of new ideas.

This has its parallels with the foundations of mathematical logic, again a creation of the Ancient Greeks, where a series of axioms of statements, combined with a set of generative rules, can be used to build the towers of mathematics. Transferred to the business context, this will later lead us to the observation that innovative companies often have a set of related tech-

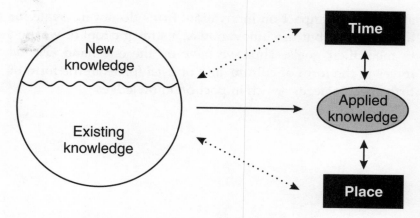

Figure 4.2 Knowledge, time and place.

nologies from which they can continually create effective innovations.

Modifiers of Knowledge: Time and Place

Knowledge is the key ingredient of innovation, but the nature of knowledge and its use are modified by two other key ingredients, time and place. These three together form the three axes on which our analysis of diversity is based.

Place, it can be hypothesized, is particularly important for cultural reasons. Companies tend to be embedded in the cultures in which they are physically located; if they are operating multi-nationally, diverse cultural influences may be at work. Different cultures, it can be further inferred, have different concepts of knowledge and learning. If innovation is based on knowledge, then cultural concepts of knowledge will impact on both the nature and processes of innovation.

Time is important for firm-specific reasons. Time refers to the concept of the corporate life cycle, and to the fact that at different stages of their evolution and growth, companies will have different needs. Strategic and operational variations must also have an impact on innovation: firms do not innovate for the sake of it, but use innovation as a strategic tool or weapon to meet their goals. Thus we have on the one hand *external* forces in the form of culture, and *internal* forces in the form of firm-specific needs which impact on knowledge.

Chapter 5

- -

Vision and Breadth:
The Nature of Innovation

Types of Innovations

The nature of innovation itself is not always clear, and there is a lack of agreement over precisely what innovation is. Frequently, innovation is thought of in terms of technologies that give rise to either new products or new processes; but this distinction seems far too narrow, and does not encompass all the diverse arenas in which innovation can take place.

A broader and at the same time more powerful approach – which is adopted in this book – is to view innovation as an activity geared towards the generation and application of new knowledge. This approach has the advantage of not getting bogged down in trying to create and distinguish functional typologies of innovation, and instead considers innovation – of whatever type – as something within the broader context of the human search for and application of knowledge. Plato was an innovator in the sphere of pure thought, as he searched for the means to order knowledge itself; Abelard sought to expand the boundaries of reason, Einstein those of our understanding of our physical surroundings and Jung those of our knowledge of the mind as an organ of thought. Each sought to advance knowledge of a particular subject, for a variety of ends or sometimes for no other end than to expand our knowledge of our world and our universe.

In business, innovation can similarly occur in many contexts and for many purposes. It can be very close to the market and be very much a market-driven process; but it can also exist almost in isolation from the market, even from the rest of the company. It can be oriented towards achieving technological excellence, excellent systems or artistic perfection. In all these cases, the nature of innovation can depend on the current phase of the corporate life cycle. And, while profitability, growth and increased value are the ultimate goals of innovation, the passion for science referred to in the previous chapter plays a role as well; innovation in business is sometimes undertaken partly out of love.

The primary connotation of innovation, and the aspect most commonly described in textbooks and management books, is technology. To many, innovation is synonymous with techno-logical advancement, which in turn means one of two things: technological improvements in *products*, or technological improvements in *processes*.

However, there are many more dimensions than this. As Porter (1990) points out, there are many varieties of innovation; seeking new *markets*, for example, could also be classed as an innovation. Nor do innovations necessarily rely on technology; they can easily be artistic and aesthetic, taking an existing product and enhancing its aesthetic features, or designing a product from scratch with the intention of setting an aesthetic standard. Versace's fashions are primarily aesthetic, though there is a technological aspect to them; Psion's computer products are designed with aesthetic appeal in mind; Microsoft has made a name by designing software that is not only technically superb but visually appealing and easy to use.

Commercialization and the Process of Innovation

One of the classic economic definitions of innovation is that of

Mansfield (1968: 99): 'An invention, when applied for the first time, is called an innovation.' An invention, says Mansfield, has little or no value until it has been applied. Innovation 'is the key stage in the process leading to the full evaluation and utilization of an invention.' Mansfield also makes the point, citing the example of Du Pont and nylon, that the inventor and the innovator can sometimes be one and the same; in this case the processes are linked but still separate. If this definition is accepted, then it paves the way for an understanding of innovation as a broad concept, encompassing not only creativity but the more general exploitation of products, processes, markets and ideas. Innovation, in this context, becomes the exploitation of knowledge. A further dimension is provided by Rothwell (1977) who makes a distinction between 'pull' innovations which are a direct response to an identifiable market demand, and 'push' innovations which come about when an innovator develops an innovation in isolation from the market. These 'push' innovations often fall out of experiments in pure science, for example.

As such, it is a complex process, and few managerial tasks are more difficult than the successful management of innovation. Innovation is both *multi-faceted* and *multi-level*. Multi-faceted in this context means that skill variety and plurality of knowledge, rather than skill homogeneity or even focused vision and single-mindedness, are the keys to enduring success in generating ideas. Ideas themselves are often inter-disciplinary or inter-functional in nature. Creative people can benefit from cross-fertilization across disciplines and a broader, cosmopolitan perspective (Cohen and Levinthal, 1990). Many innovative firms tend to structure innovative processes so as to draw together people from different backgrounds with different knowledge and skill sets; the 'knowledge crew' described in Japanese firms is one version of this. It is necessary here to distinguish between invention, which is often an individual effort, and innovation, which is the result of a collective achievement. Although an innovation may have its origin in one part of a unit, other parts may play an

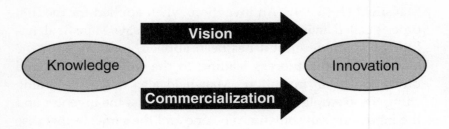

Figure 5.1 Knowledge to innovation

important role in idea realization and commercialization; an example can be seen in the Norwegian firm Norsk Hydro, which passed one particular product innovation through a number of different departments over the course of a seven year period, looking for the right application. Multiple functions and disciplines are frequently required to transform an idea into reality.

Plato's Concepts Applied to Innovation

There is a simple correlation between the three Platonic ideals and innovation. All innovations can be roughly divided into three types: those which seek excellence through aesthetic appeal, those which seek excellence through management innovations, and those which seek excellence through scientific discovery or technological advancement.

Aesthetic innovations appeal to consumers through their senses: a car with graceful elegant lines, a music CD of a very fine performance of a symphony, a silk fabric which is appealing to touch, perhaps even a meal which smells and tastes better than the ordinary; or, frequently, a combination of several of these features. In the past, Europe has been a leader in aesthetic products, and even today with innovation in Europe apparently lagging behind, European firms such as

Jaguar, Vuitton, Rolex and Christian Dior are bywords for aesthetic excellence.

Management innovation usually refers to innovations such as new processes or new markets. These can be seen to provide benefits such as efficiency, effectiveness, value and profitability. A streamlined production facility using CAD-CAM and automated production lines, for example, would be an innovation aimed at achieving goodness. Japanese firms, with their strong emphasis on the socialization of knowledge, tend to typify this type of innovation more than do European firms. On the whole, European firms have been criticized for neglecting this aspect of innovation, but there are many exceptions: Michelin, for example, is a leader in this area.

Technological advancement is the form of innovation which is most commonly discussed, and refers to the translation of new scientific or technical discoveries into advanced products. Examples here might be a car that runs particularly well or efficiently, or Michelin's 'green' radial tyre which produces fuel economy benefits for motorists. Pharmaceuticals can represent breakthrough products with huge impacts; examples include insulin and penicillin. Computers, software, electronics and instruments as well as more low-tech products such as soap, and services such as banking and financial services can partake of technological advancement. On the whole European firms have an excellent record of developing new technologies, but their performance in bringing these successfully to market has been more uneven.

It should be noted, of course, that innovations do not usually fit neatly into one of these three spheres. In many cases, technology, aesthetics and management go hand in hand, and elements of all three are necessary to bring innovations to market. One can take for example the Italian fashion and design firm Versace, which, though its products are rooted firmly in aesthetic appeal, has nonetheless used technological sophistication on a variety of levels coupled with a strong management structure to achieve market success. Michelin, as mentioned

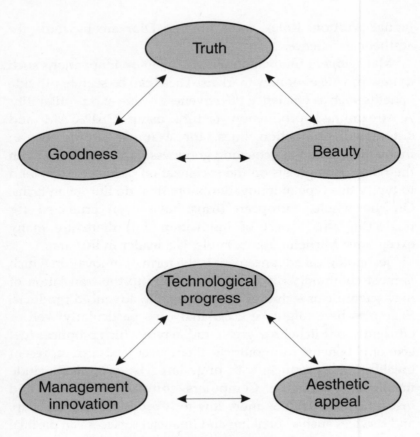

Figure 5.2 Platonic innovation spheres

above, has used both technological inventiveness and management innovation to become a leader in its field.

Innovation and Time

Finally, referring once again to Mansfield, innovation is
strongly time dependent. The diffusion of innovation is an
important economic factor. How long will it take for a given
innovation to become accepted? Equally importantly, how long
will it be before rivals copy the innovation and use it as a
competitive weapon against the firm?

The executives of innovative firms, therefore, must operate in two time dimensions. First, they have to manage on a day-to-day basis; second they have to take a long view (and in some fields, this means a very long view, five, ten or more years) and plan the innovations of the future. It is the latter, of course, which is the most difficult, particularly today when there is a general lack of clarity about (and confidence in) the future (Füredi, 1992). Managers today are only too aware that the future is unpredictable and uncertain, yet, if they are to innovate, they have to face the future and attempt to plan for it.

How far firms look forward depends to some extent on what stage of the corporate life cycle they currently occupy. Current literature on this subject identifies three key stages.

In the first stage, often associated with business start-ups, firms are concerned with the immediate exploitation of good ideas. Often this idea has been the genesis of the firm itself, which has been established for the purpose of exploitation. Examples in our study include Psion and Microsoft, established to exploit the technological inventions of David Potter and Bill Gates, and Bertelsmann, founded by Carl Bertelsmann with a view to satisfying a perceived need for educational products; the first two can be seen as 'push' innovations while the second can be described as a 'pull' innovation.

The second stage, elaboration, is more complex. Here the firm has been successful in first stage exploitation and now needs to develop its markets, defend against competition and protect its position while simultaneously developing a new tranche of innovations and preparing them for market. By this time, it can be assumed that the firm's rivals have copied and even improved on the original innovation from stage one, and the firm must be able to prepare new innovations in order to protect its position, let increase value and profitability. The elaboration stage is sometimes a painful one, and there are many traps for the unwary innovator. In our study, Psion and Trumpf are examples of firms which ran into trouble in the elaboration stage and had to respond rapidly to new threats.

Finally, orientation is the stage where the firm, now strongly established, contemplates the future and plans how it will use its innovative capabilities to meet challenges and create opportunities. This is the visionary stage, and as will be discussed in Section 4, it requires a special kind of leadership. Economics are important, but passion, vision and morality can be equally important in the formulation of vision. Successful Japanese firms such as Kao and Sharp usually possess visionary leaders; in Europe, Mondragón, Salomon, Michelin and Bertelsmann are examples of companies in the visionary, orientation stage.

The Many Paths of Innovation

Innovation is a complex and diverse phenomenon. It can be directed at products, processes, markets or other business activities. It can be founded on technological inventions, but equally it can relate to aesthetic or social ideals. It is multi-faceted, in that many skills and many kinds of vision can contribute to the innovation process; it is multi-level, in that many different people at different levels can contribute to the process. Finally, the nature of innovation will depend on the corporate life cycle; the stages of creation, elaboration and orientation call for different visions of innovation. Truly, there is no one best way to innovate; a wide variety of circumstances influences the innovation process.

This multi-faceted nature of innovation is an opportunity, for it greatly widens the arena to which the creative use of knowledge – of innovation – can be applied, and it widens the responsibility to innovate away from those managers responsible for, say, R&D, to all who have the possibility of changing some aspect of their business.

Chapter 6

- -

Time Past, Time Future:
The Imperative of
Innovation

(лишительной) необходимой

We will never be asked whether we want a given historical development.

Max Weber

Like it or not, the past infects the world we live in, the decisions we make, the very choices we see to lie before us. If we ignore its influence, we do not escape its power. All we do is remain to some extent its prisoners without ever really knowing that is what we are. If, however, we acknowledge it, learn to recognize its workings, come to greet it on familiar terms, we can put it to excellent use.

Alan M. Kantrow, *The Constraints of Corporate Tradition*

For centuries, Europe enjoyed technological and economic superiority over the rest of the globe. The roots of this superiority lay in science, evolved by the Greeks and handed down to modern Europe through the Romans and the Arabs. The Romans, though great administrators, were largely elaborators of the Greek scientific tradition; innovation was not a Roman priority. The story is told of the Emperor Hadrian giving an audience to an engineer who had designed a mechanical dredge for clearing harbours, an operation currently carried out by hand using thousands of paid labourers. Hadrian thanked the inventor and rewarded him but refused to adopt the invention; had he done so, he said, the thousands of labourers would have been out of work. The idea that these labourers might have been put to more useful work elsewhere does not seem to have occurred.

Eventually Rome became nothing more than a vast bureaucracy, static and with a diminishing economic base, and thus it fell. The Arabs, widely credited with inheriting and advancing Greek science and learning in the first six centuries after the Hegira, took over the mantle of leadership in a large portion of the world; military conquest was followed by economic establishment and scientific progress, and for a time the Arab cultures were the most technically advanced in the world. In the end, however, the Arabs lost their predominance because, for a variety of cultural and political reasons, they failed to learn as fast as their European neighbours and rivals. As described in the prologue, from the twelfth century Renaissance onwards Europe developed a culture which was centred on scientific, technical and philosophical advancement; and it was only a matter of time before these advances translated into economic – and political – domination. The near simultaneous opening of seagoing trade routes to Asia and America, the old cultures to the east and the new world to the west, heralded that translation. Both America, the offspring of Europe, and Japan, which began belatedly in the late nineteenth century to catch up with Europe, were strongly affected by and influenced by European models of innovation and knowledge.

As the twentieth century draws to close, the imperative of innovation is stronger than ever. As the information revolution shrinks the globe and opens new markets to multitudes of new competitors, a company's knowledge is one of the few competitive advantages over which it can maintain control. In Europe this imperative is becoming particularly strong. If

European companies and economies are to survive and prosper against world competition, they will need to revive those historic innovative strengths.

Innovation is the *sine qua non* prerequisite for competitive advantage. Porter (1990: 45) comments that 'Firms create competitive advantage by perceiving or discovering new and better ways to compete in an industry and bring them to market, which is ultimately an act of innovation.' He adds that although firms can also sometimes gain advantage through imitation (for example, through low-cost strategies), such advantage is seldom lasting. In our study, the importance ascribed to innovation could be found in the 'innovate, don't imitate' philosophies of leaders as diverse as Tokuji Hayakawa, Bill Gates, Georges Salomon and Gianni Versace.

De Geus (1988) has commented that in the near future, if not already, a company's single sustainable competitive advantage is its ability to learn faster than its competitors. Learning in this case means innovation; it is not enough merely to learn, the resulting knowledge must also be put into effect.

competitive advantage

Chapter 7

The Character of Successful Innovative Companies

After three thousand years of explosion, by means of fragmentary and mechanical technologies, the Western world is imploding. . . . After more than a century of electric technology, we have extended our central nervous system itself in a global embrace, abolishing both space and time so far as our planet is concerned.

Marshall McLuhan, *Understanding Media*

Introduction

This chapter looks at innovative companies around the world, with particular reference to the thirteen companies profiled in our study, with a view to developing the groundwork on global success factors required for the following chapters. The existence of these global success factors is both factual and important, and should not be obscured by the emphasis on diversity throughout this book. One of the most intriguing results of the thirteen case studies was the fact that many of the apparent differences in organization and practice between firms turned out on closer inspection to be similarities.

Companies of vastly different origin or size turn out to not only have very similar attitudes to innovation but also use very similar organizational structures and strategies to achieve innovation and creativity.

The presence of these common elements is important. By looking at examples of other organizations which have been successful innovators and trying to replicate those processes within their own organizations, firms can become more innovative themselves; much as painters study the work of other painters in order to learn techniques, which become the foundation of their own particular style. The masters of European painting have nearly all learned their craft by studying the works of their predecessors and contemporaries; many were even pupils of other masters. One of the key arguments of this book is that companies should seek out other innovative companies, learn what these companies do well and then learn lessons which can be applied to their own companies. It is thus useful to begin by looking at fundamental similarities in terms of success factors, particularly those which appear at the global level.

David and Goliath: Microsoft and IBM in the USA

Microsoft, the world's leading producer of computer software products, has become a legend in its time. Fundamental to Microsoft's current success has been its ability to attract, select and develop talented individuals. In the words of founder and president Bill Gates, 'we're in the intellectual property business', and from the company's earliest days, the constant need to develop new and better products made hiring top talent, as well as quickly bringing individual contributions on-line, a top priority. Again to quote Gates:

We've always had the most aggressive approach of any software company in finding people with top IQs and bringing them in. We also pushed to the absolute limit the people we brought in from overseas. Finally, we designed a development methodology that could make use of different individuals' talents.

Creating an Intensely Competitive Atmosphere

Hiring and developing talented individuals was critical but not sufficient for Microsoft. The company needed not only to develop such people but also to place them in circumstances where each would excel. As such, Microsoft has tried to retain the feel of a small firm, with an informal but intensely competitive atmosphere. 'The Microsoft style is pretty aggressive', remarked one manager. 'People jump on each other all the time. But it's not personal. It's a challenging, aggressive style.' Stories abound of combative meetings and 'yelling matches' between groups of software developers, each advocating new features for coming products. Critical e-mail messages, often sarcastic or sharp in tone, are known around the company as 'flame mail'. The overall tone, then, is not only informal but also profoundly pragmatic and achievement oriented.

Establishing Personal Responsibility

To reinforce such an achievement orientation, Microsoft's compensation policy has continued to emphasize employee participation in the company's fortunes. In addition to salaries, which remain somewhat below industry levels, new employees receive a sizeable stock grant. The company's philosophy of personal responsibility is further emphasized by a management accounting system which fosters visibility and accountability. All revenues and costs, identified by product and by sales channel, are fed into a single consolidated ledger; this database is then exploded into many profit and loss statements, each focusing on a particular business unit, marketing channel or geographical area. Actual sales and expense figures can be reviewed on-line, resulting in high visibility and individual accountability. Profitability is not the province of 'someone in

HQ', but the responsibility of everyone. As one software developer commented:

> One of the reasons our products are so successful is that everybody takes responsibility for them. You own this thing; you make it great; you're responsible for it. . . . Your input is taken seriously. It doesn't matter what level you're at or where you are, you compete like hell for the business.

Remaining Forever Competitive

Personal accountability, therefore, is reinforced by a competitive orientation. In Bill Gates' words:

> Each business unit is focused on its competition. We have a Spreadsheet Business Unit – they wake up every morning thinking about Lotus. We have a Word Processing Business Unit – they wake up thinking about Wordperfect. We have a Networking Business Unit and they wake up thinking about Novell. Those are very entrenched competitors and we're going to have to develop far better products in order to dislodge them. We're not going to back off competing.

In the last analysis, Gates explained, success is based on deploying more individual talent within the organization than the competition. 'Once you let mediocre people into the organization, particularly at very high levels, that's going to replicate itself and you won't be a world class organization any more.' This is a lesson Microsoft may have learnt from IBM in its prime, one which also differentiates the individualistic Americans from their group-oriented Japanese competitors.

Turning David into Goliath

IBM, in the 1970s and 1980s, had the same charisma and status in the United States as Microsoft has had in the 1990s. Its difficulties at the end of the 1980s, however, should not serve

Microsoft: informality, creativity and tension

Microsoft was founded by two computer programmers, Bill Gates and a former school classmate, Paul Allen. Their first achievement was to implement the computer language BASIC for the Altair microcomputer in 1974. The company's primary product focus has continued to be on software and operating systems for PCs, and its products MS-DOS and Windows have become virtually world standards for PC manufacturers. In 1994 the company's revenues were $ 4.6 billion.

Fundamental to Microsoft's success has been its ability to attract, select, develop and retain people. Recognizing that personal skills and attitudes are crucial in the software business, Microsoft has concentrated hard on providing the right kind of sustaining and creative corporate culture. In the words of Gates, 'we nurture an atmosphere in which creative thinking thrives and employees develop to their fullest potential.' Styles are informal – employees can and do communicate directly with Gates by e-mail, for example – but at the same time the atmosphere is intense. Product development meetings are often highly combative. However, the conflicts are less to do with personal rivalry than with an intense desire to 'get it right'; in the final analysis, all that really matters is that the product works.

Bill Gates continues to play a key role in product development, but is no longer immediately involved in the actual development process. Instead, Gates and his top managers identify new product needs and then coordinate and control product research teams who are charged with bringing new products into being. This demands both a high degree of central control and a very strong leadership ability, attributes which the entrepreneurial Gates is well able to bring to his company.

to conceal the overall impact and innovative reputation of this American colossus. In order to foster innovation the company's founder, Thomas J. Watson, and his successors (notably his son, Thomas Watson, Jr) created a work environment that both respected the individual and instilled strongly shared corporate values. 'Think' signs were placed conspicuously around the company, internal competition was fervently cultivated, and nonconformist 'wild geese' were – at least in the early days – strongly promoted. Paradoxically, however, particularly since the mid-1980s, it is the introduction of a cult of conformity, as opposed to both individuality and also familiarity, that has

---

IBM: technological prowess fails to reach markets

In 1914, Thomas J. Watson joined the Computing, Tabulating and Recording Company; ten years later, as its president, he changed the company to International Business Machines. Under his stewardship and that of his son, Thomas J. Watson, Jr, IBM became the largest computer corporation in the world; in 1989 its revenues reached $62 billion.

Throughout its history, IBM's track record as an innovative company has been exceptional. R&D spending has often been as much as 10 per cent of annual revenues; the 1990 figure was $6.6 billion. The company has research labs and facilities in many parts of the world, and in 1986 two IBM researchers in the Zurich laboratory received the Nobel Prize for their invention of the scanning tunnelling microscope. IBM sees constant innovation as a key strategy for staying ahead of its competitors, and believes that its huge size and the enormous resources devoted to innovation give it a competitive edge. In 1982, IBM was identified by Tom Peters and Robert Waterman as one of America's best-run companies, largely on the strength of its ability to innovate and bring new products to market.

By 1990, however, IBM was in trouble and by 1992 large losses were being incurred. The trouble was that, despite its obvious commitment to and belief in innovation, IBM had developed a corporate structure which impeded or prevented innovations reaching the market. Technological and engineering prowess was not being converted into sales and profit. Ironing out these structural problems will be the major task facing IBM over the next decade.

---

pulled the company down. IBM missed a succession of opportunities in the development of both hardware and software products, and in the latter case this paved the way for Microsoft's ultimate success.

So IBM in the 1990s has (perhaps temporarily) lost sight of the American dream. Respect for the individual in the context of the IBM family had been crushed by the weight of the bureaucracy, pulled down by IBM conformity. There was no co-operative group to mediate between the individual and the organization. In the process, risk-taking enterprise had been suppressed by risk-avoiding bureaucracy. While IBM, the east coast American Goliath, had fallen, Microsoft, the west coast American David, had risen.

Focusing on Utility: Psion in the UK

Psion is Europe's leading producer of hand-held computers. The focus on innovation in this company is coupled with an orientation towards utility. From the outset, or almost so, Psion had a leaning towards sophistication, cleverly combining physical science with competent engineering. It is also interesting to compare and contrast its approach with that of Sharp:

> Sharp's products look to be better value than ours, at first glance, but actually they're quite shallow. We go for depths that belie first appearances. When I first joined the company I bought the Organizer product and was amazed at the depth of application. It's our intellectual background, and we believe in true utility. Simplicity, functionality, depth. We're good at materialization. We build products for ourselves, and for our fans, and we are generalists. At the same time we tend to take a rifle shot approach, going for particular targets; the Japanese take a buck shot approach, spraying out the ammunition to see what hits.

This analytical focus underlies the company's attitude to relationships, and stands in contrast to the networked approach used by other firms. Unlike in the Japanese case, moreover, Psion has been unable to sustain harmonious and productive relationships with its UK suppliers. During its most recent transition period in the early 1990, Psion brought its manufacturing in house; this proved necessary because, among other things, the company was unable to achieve the quality standards that it required – as a technological innovator – out of house.

Fostering Innovation

For Psion's founder David Potter:

> The computer is unique because, unlike a pen or a car, it is

not an end in itself. The hardware itself does not do anything. It needs software for that. Therefore a good computer product is one that can accommodate thousands of potential applications, each one of which can enable particular customers to their problems.

Historically, therefore, there has been a strong emphasis at Psion on technological innovation. Only lip service has been paid to a market-driven approach. Recently, however, the emphasis has begun to change and the company is having more contact with retailers. The reason, in effect, is that these retailers expect leading edge technology from Psion. 'We live in a world of continuing turmoil and flux', Potter stresses. 'Controlled chaos. You have to undergo flux to survive'. Psion had been changing from 8 bit to 16 bit and then to 32 bit computing over a period of some ten years, and everything has had to be re-engineered. 'It's been like – if we use an aircraft analogy – moving from piston to jet engines.'

Remaining Independently Minded

At the same time Psion, like its independently minded founder, reflects the 'free market' environment in which most British (and American) firms operate. Not only is the business largely independent of David Potter's own family, but it is also largely disconnected from the UK's socio-political context. While Psion is quoted on the stock market, and while the company has had recruitment links with well known UK-based universities – most particularly with Cambridge University and Imperial College – it has by now severed most of its links with UK suppliers. Moreover, while based in north London, it has little relationship with its local community.

Furthermore Psion, or at least David Potter himself, places relatively little emphasis on the network of suppliers and distributors in which the company is, therefore, apparently very loosely embedded. In fact these networks of inter-firm relationships are all but taken for granted, and are generally relegated to the lower echelons of the company's management. David Potter's role, therefore, in relation to what Nonaka might term the 'externalization of Psion's interests', is essentially that of a 'western' figurehead and not that of an 'eastern style' catalyst and facilitator.

Stimulating Aggressive Teamwork

There is a creative tension within Psion between the individual and the group. Potter himself remains an outstanding individual within the company, but he can only be effective when carrying the consensus of the group. That element is replicated within the organization as a whole, as described by R&D director Charles Davies:

> As a group we don't suffer fools gladly. There's a strong natural authority operating here. People know who the respected people are, and it's for their knowledge and skill rather than for their position. We maintain a strong intellectual environment. It's a combative culture. At the same time we've always teamed well. Like natives hunting a lion. Aggressive, but definitely a team. Americans have the rock star syndrome. The technical guru in sandals in the middle of things. We have a core team. Anybody is free to express their opinion but they won't be listened to until they've won their spurs. We're a consensus culture, but intolerant of people who don't buy in.

In that context, there are many parallels between Psion and Microsoft, reflecting perhaps a greater similarity between America and Britain than between the former and other European cultures.

Balancing Freedom and Order

Potter has clearly been intent on establishing a Psion identity that serves to heal one of the great divides in the British national psyche. As such, he has been balancing freedom (through play and creativity) with order (through planning and organization), again something akin to what is happening at Microsoft. In so doing, moreover, Potter is attempting to bring together the freedom-loving, eccentric strain in British society with the conservative, establishment characteristics. The result, in Potter's view, is a company dedicated to creative engineering:

> We believe profoundly in creativity, and in play. But it's a tough world out there. Unless you realize that, you will perish. Development people need to create, but not in a vacuum. In fact they're much happier working within a framework. Planning is not inconsistent with creativity. Good engineering results in quality and value, which has been creatively developed and meticulously implemented. It involves producing things of use to people that work, which are cost-effective, which don't break down, which have quality about them. That sounds pragmatic enough for Anglo-Saxon purposes!

America, Japan and Europe

Yet the culture with which Psion management as a whole identify is more European than English, and this general orientation towards 'European-ness' is reinforced by the spread of Anglo-Saxons and Celts amongst Psion's senior personnel, as well as by its strong market positioning in Europe:

> I'd say we're a European company. In Europe Psion is first in the palmtop market, followed by Sharp and by HP. Our products, unlike the Japanese and American ones, are localized. We produce them in the local European language. The Americans want something that's 'man for the job'; the Japanese like something intricate and aesthetic. We Europeans are something in between.

Despite their varied geographical origins (including South

Psion: the independent visionary

Psion is best-known for its hand-held computers but is also a major designer and manufacturer of systems software. The company was founded in 1980 by David Potter, a Zimbabwean-born engineer and academic. Potter began by supplying software to computer hardware manufacturers such as Sinclair and Acorn, but when these ran into trouble Psion began developing new products, most famously the 'Organizer' handheld database machine.

Psion is led from the top by a small team of intensely dedicated people, who are in turn led by Potter himself. Potter combines in equal parts hard-headed business acumen, engineering and design skills, strong independence and an almost romantic vision of the possibilities of science. Although the firm places considerable importance on the development of networks of both suppliers and customers, these networks are loose and constantly changing; for example, the company is at present switching away from outsourcing components to making a higher proportion in-house.

Organization and creative flux are represented in equal parts in Psion. Planning and creativity are both stressed, and are not seen as contradictory. This company is an excellent example of a top-down driven entrepreneurial company, distinctive and eccentric on the one hand, yet innovative and thoroughly professional on the other.

Africa and Hong Kong), Potter and his people feel themselves to be distinctly European (at least, up to a point). As an organization, Psion has remained somewhat ambivalent in its cultural orientation. As we have seen, Psion generally conceives of itself as European, being influenced by an overall cultural affinity with the continent and a strong commercial presence in France, Germany, Italy and the Benelux countries. However, in technological terms, Potter has greatest admiration for the Japanese and psychologically his R&D people are oriented towards America:

Psion buys a lot from Japan, Korea and Taiwan. Yet as far as development is concerned, Psion is quite American. Psion's development people come to work in jeans and tee-shirts, and they read Dr Dobbs' *Calisthenetics*, published in California. At the same time, though, Psion is otherwise very European. It's not confrontational and contractual, like the Americans; rather people sit around a table and come to an agreement, co-operatively.

It is here that Psion fundamentally parts company from its collaborators and competitors across the Atlantic.

Pursuing Service, Truth and Egalitarianism: Kao and Sharp in Japan

In Japan, by way of contrast, large-scale manufacturing enterprises, as exemplified here by traditionally oriented Kao and by modern day Sharp, remain alive and well. Kao has developed a distinctive management philosophy that is both very similar and very different to that of IBM. The company's traditional business dates back to 1890 when Tomio Nagase founded Kao Soap. The soap industry seemed highly promising at the time, as the Japanese people's lifestyle was being rapidly modernized. Most domestic soap was cheap, but quality was quite low. Believing that 'a clean nation prospers', Nagase aimed to produce high-quality soap. For more than a century thereafter Kao has conducted its business following Tomio Nagase's belief that 'cleanliness is the best way of advancing a nation and its people'. Meanwhile, as the business has diversified into cosmetics and floppy disks, it has adopted an enriched corporate slogan: 'cleanliness, health and beauty'. In the late twentieth century, Kao's president Yoshio Maruta created a new management philosophy, duly summarized in three principles: (1) service to the customer; (2) the search for truth; and (3) absolute egalitarianism.

The first principle, *service to the customer*, means that Kao's primary purpose is not to earn profits or gain market share but to offer joy and satisfaction to customers through products manufactured to suit their needs. As Maruta has said:

> Kao's ultimate goal is to embody our knowledge into our customer products. It is to serve consumers according to the mercy advocated by Queen Srimala, a pious Buddhist in ancient India. . . . In sum we should not force our products on consumers, but always think from their points of view.

Fumikazu Tokiwa, who in 1994 succeeded Maruta as president, makes this precise definition: the consumer does not buy a price, the consumer buys values.

The second principle, *search for the truth*, reflects Kao's emphasis on teamwork, not respect for the individual, drawing upon the so called laws of the universe. The search for truth is epitomized by Tokiwa, who is known for being relentless in asking 'Why?' Again, in the words of Maruta:

> The wisdom of a corporation does not come from its top management but from the amassed knowledge of all of its members. . . . The long-range prosperity of a corporation depends on whether it can accumulate this knowledge and accumulate it into one.

The third and final principle of *absolute equality* implies that all of Kao's organizational members must be treated as equals so that a business institution can be established in which the best use is made of everyone's opinions. Accordingly, and believing that unequal access to information is a major source of authoritarianism, Kao has developed a completely open information system, that serves to materialize its business philosophy.

Three major factors, in turn, have affected the development of Maruta's management philosophy. First is his profound interest in, and knowledge of, Buddhist philosophy. The second influence has been the late Eizo Ito, fourth president of Kao, who was Maruta's mentor. Although Ito married the founder's niece, he believed that Kao's family interests should be subordinated to the modernization of the company, whereby employees were promoted on the basis of merit. Rather than Kao being a family-controlled firm it needed to become, in itself, one big family. Maruta, as one such employee, shared Ito's interests in eastern philosophy, on the one hand, and western business practice, on the other. The third major influence on Maruta was its large American competitor, Procter and Gamble. When he visited the United States in the 1950s, Maruta was particularly impressed by P&G's automated mass production systems, its quality control methods, its analytically based marketing management and its public relations activities.

Building upon Knowledge Grounds

To attain its ideal of 'cleanliness, health and beauty', Kao has placed R&D at the centre of its corporate strategy. To that end the company has located its knowledge grounds in five scientific areas: fat and oil science, surface science, polymer science, biological science and applied physics. Kao aims to be the leader in each of these by accumulating both basic knowledge and applied technologies. In the process, the company investigates 'key phenomena', 'key chemicals' and 'key technologies'. At the same time, Kao has adopted five principles of product development, so that a new product must: (1) be of true benefit to society; (2) use creative technologies; (3) surpass competitors products on both price and performance; (4) pass consumer tests before market introduction; and (5) show distinctiveness in one way or another. In effect the company places as much emphasis on marketing as it does on research and development.

Becoming Bio-functional

This integral combination of R&D and marketing is carried out in what Maruta has termed a 'bio-functional organization'.

Kao: a philosophy of wisdom

'Cleanliness, health and beauty' is one of the mottos of Kao, which was founded as a soap company in 1890. Soaps and detergents remain a major product line, but the company has also diversified into product lines as diverse as paper products, cosmetics and floppy disks.

Yoshio Maruta, who retired as chairman in 1990 on the occasion of the company's centenary, has played a major role in the company's rise over the last four decades. A visionary and philosopher, Maruta established a corporate philosophy based on three principles: (1) serving the customer, (2) absolute equality of all people and (3) the search for truth and the unity of wisdom. At Kao, the combined knowledge of all employees has more importance than the genius of one individual. Fumikazu Tokiwa, who succeeded Maruta as president, emphasizes the values, meanings and joys of sharing knowledge and participating in innovation for all employees. Every employee has something to contribute to the knowledge base, but no one person has primacy.

Kao relies heavily on vertically-integrated, 'origin-oriented' research and development to bring products to market. Vertical integration allows tighter control, both in terms of cost reduction and influencing product development. 'Origin-oriented' means that research is heavily focused on basics, on the 'origin of things'. Tokiwa stands for a curiousness in science and in people. He became one of the youngest leaders in Kao's history of the household research centre. New chemicals or compounds are discovered first, and new materials products and applications are then developed. The result is a company with a high degree of technological dominance, where core scientific work provides the impulse for the constant development and improvement of products.

Such an organization is one in which 'we look at the organization as a single living organism, though it is comprised of many people. In such an organization all members know what the others are doing or thinking and can immediately join hands and work together'. In other words, the bio-functional organization is something like a human body which can naturally heal itself of a disease or injury through the simultaneous reactions of all organs. Likewise, all departments of the bio-functional organization quickly react to problems without receiving directions from above.

In fact senior management meetings at Kao are open to all employees who are either generally interested in the topic, or have a specific proposal to make in relation to it. Similarly, an R&D conference held every month at each one of the four corporate laboratories, is open to all comers. Furthermore, Kao has promoted intensive communications between each of its 18 divisions through the extensive use of network of 3800 computers. Finally, twice a year new product development meetings are held in five major cities across Japan, which are attended by members of all departments. 'Our voltage reaches its highest level on two occasions . . . energy abounds. . . . There is a rhythm, a flow of concentrated energy.' Ultimately, moreover, its R&D departments are considered to be a reservoir of human resources. This is even more the case at Sharp Electronics.

Towards the Knowledge-creating Company

In order to pursue the creative philosophy first established by Tokuji Hayakawa, Sharp has since developed a unique organizational structure, geared towards the 'knowledge society'. Knowledge in the form of new technologies and products is created through the effective use of three layers: a business system that is hierarchical and functionally departmentalized; project teams that are organized flexibly for developing new products; and a knowledge base comprised of tacit and explicit knowledge. Important product development projects are organized under an 'Urgent Project System', with project teams independent of Sharp's R&D laboratories. Every member of such teams wears a gold badge (this system also means that a department may be deprived of its best people for up to a year). In 1985, a new Lifestyle Centre was created in response to social changes that were perceived to be arising in society; products were systematized from stand-alone products into product groups that reflected particular lifestyles. Takaji

---

Sharp: a knowledge society

In 1912, Tokuji Hayakawa, an inventor and innovator who designed the ever-sharp pencil, set up his first metalworks in Tokyo. In the 1920s, relocating to Osaka after the great earthquake of 1923, Hayakawa began producing radios and electrical equipment and renamed his firm Hayakawa Electric Industries. Today the firm, renamed Sharp in honour of Hayakawa's most famous invention, is one of the largest and most respected electronics firms in the world.

The history of Sharp is built on innovation. Hayakawa told his employees 'Don't imitate. Make something that others want to imitate.' Over the years since the Second World War, Sharp has been a pioneer in fields such as televisions, electronic calculators, liquid crystal displays and opto-electronics. When, as in the case of electronic calculators, competition has threatened its market position, Sharp has relied on innovative products and product features to put clear water between it and its competitors.

Within the company there is what might be termed a 'knowledge society', in which knowledge and innovation are omnipresent. All levels of the company, corporate, business group and business division, have their own R&D labs with different levels of responsibility; in addition, Sharp uses a flexible system of project groups which can if necessary step outside the corporate hierarchy to develop specific innovations. At Sharp, knowledge and the ability to turn knowledge into innovation have been hardwired into the corporate culture.

Ohgawara, a former director of the centre, characterized the organization as a 'guerrilla force against conventional concepts'.

When comparing the corporate cultures of Microsoft and IBM with those of Kao and Sharp, we become aware of the basic differentiation between an American orientation (personal/individual) and a Japanese (collective/group) orientation. At the same time, it is important to recognize, most overtly in the Kao case, how the prevailing corporate culture was able to accommodate its 'shadow', exemplified by Procter & Gamble. In Kao's case, the company learned a great deal from P&G in terms of marketing.

Rationality, Precision and Accuracy: Trumpf and Bertelsmann in Germany

While small scale enterprise flourishes in Anglo-Saxon cultures, Germany is noted for its medium-sized, family-owned concerns. Trumpf is one such; Trumpf is to machine tools in Germany what Psion is to mobile computers in the UK.

Today Trumpf, more than seventy years after it was founded by Christian Trumpf, develops and produces machine tools for sheet-metal working, punching presses, electrical tools and laser equipment. In the field of laser technology it is an industry leader. The main production sites are in Germany where the company employs 2000 of its 3000 employees. The Trumpf philosophy is communicated through a logo that is comprised of a simple blue square, associated with rationality, precision and accuracy. This is embodied in the rationally based, technological orientation of the current chairman, Dr Berthold Leibinger: 'I am heavily involved in determining the general direction of our research and development. There is no area that our R&D director does not talk to me about.' Technik, it would seem, is all!

Diligence, Engineering and Politeness

The cultural environment of Germany's south-west, with its pietistic focus on rationality, cleanliness and precision, has heavily influenced Trumpf, together with other firms such as Daimler Benz and Porsche. As noted in the previous chapter, this region of south-western Germany is well known for its large number of flourishing, medium-sized firms. Respect for authority and technical competence, unremitting diligence and infinite politeness are therefore a central feature of Trumpf culture, and indeed of that of Mercedes Benz or Porsche.

At the same time Trumpf is heavily influenced by Japan. Both Dr Leibinger himself, whose mother traded in Far Eastern works of art, and his son-in-law, the production director, have spent many years in that country. In Leibinger's words 'I have always admired the Japanese for their devotion to the task, their eagerness and politeness.'

This mix of German and Japanese elements might serve to explain the somewhat paradoxical relationship between leadership and delegation at Trumpf. Leibinger is very much of a paternalist, or even an autocrat, albeit a benevolent one. 'I believe in the necessity of authority in life. My ideal is to be an enlightened patriarch, someone who is responsible for a task and who knows that he must care for others, and who is aware that he is dependent on others.' We see here a mixture of northern dependence and eastern interdependence.

Competence, Technik and Paternalism

Close supervision and guidance in the company is instilled through both personal and also technocratic measures of co-ordination, within each of the functional areas of the business. At the same time, more recently, a 'management by projects' system has been introduced. These incorporate clear objective setting among project teams; close co-operation between project team members; clear definition of responsibilities; a competence based approach to the allocation of such responsibilities; and finally co-ordinated interdependence between functional areas.

Two criteria play important roles in Trumpf's selection and development of its personnel. Firstly, employees are required to have an excellent education in relevant areas of science and technology. Secondly, all employees are expected to have internalized the values which form the very basis of Trumpf's corporate culture. These are unpretentiousness, a sense of duty, a strong performance orientation, as well as self-confidence coupled with unselfishness.

Until recently Trumpf had an implicit policy of lifetime employment. Having been forced to lay off people in the 1990s, the company reduced the 'shock effect' by effectively cutting wages so that staff cuts could be minimized. The earnings of high-level employees were in the process reduced more

---

Trumpf: technology at the top

Trumpf GmbH & Co. is a leading German machine tool maker, concentrating on cutting edge technology such as laser machine tools. The company was founded in Ditzingen, Germany, by Christian Trumpf in 1923; in 1994 the firm recorded a turnover of DM 624 million. The current chairman is Dr Berthold Leibinger, an engineer who developed a machine tool which was the basis of the company's growth in the 1960s and 1970s; Dr Leibinger also owns 75 per cent of Trumpf shares.

Although Trumpf is an international company, R&D remains tightly concentrated in Germany. Hans Klingel, the vice-president who is second in line to Dr Leibinger, has direct responsibility for innovation. Key features of Trumpf include a very high R&D (8 per cent of turnover in 1993–4), constant development of new products to maintain a competitive edge, co-operative links with technical and research centres, and a human resources policy that stresses education and internal promotion and development.

Trumpf is also deeply embedded in its own regional culture, that of Swabia in south-west Germany. Pietistic values such as unselfishness, devotion, diligence and eagerness to work are central elements of Trumpf's corporate culture. As one engineer explained: 'You can't just work an eight hour day and then go home; you would feel guilty.'

---

drastically than those of blue-collar workers. Moreover, the good relationship that management had with its works council helped to smooth the transition. Finally, the pietistic values of unselfish devotion to the company and diligence to the organizational cause militates against performance related pay. Bertelsmann, based in northern Germany, is different.

Enterprise, Responsibility and Partnership

Bertelsmann, originally founded in 1824, only began its growth and development into a world-wide media enterprise after the war. Where Trumpf is technical Bertelsmann is entrepreneurial, though both are firmly lodged within society. This dates back, for Bertelsmann, to the personal involvement of Reinhard Mohn, who restarted the business after the war, having been positively impressed by concepts of personal responsibility and

---

Bertelsmann: dynamic bureaucracy
and managerial freedom
·································

Until the Time–Warner merger in 1989, Bertelsmann AG was the largest media corporation in the world. Founded in 1824 by Carl Bertelsmann, the company took off after the Second World War under the leadership of the entrepreneur Reinhard Mohn, and over the last four decades it has enjoyed an average annual growth rate of 10 per cent. The company has operations in forty countries in sectors such as printing, publishing and broadcast media. 1994 turnover was DM 18.4 billion.

Technological complexity is not a feature of the Bertelsmann product range. The focus of innovation lies instead in the field of innovative business concepts and management systems, which have in turn been the key to the company's phenomenal growth. Reinhard Mohn's legacy has been a culture of individual responsibility and entrepreneurship combined with a strong sense of social responsibility and partnership.

In Bertelsmann, reference is not made to 'managers' or 'management'. The company is run not by bureaucrats but by entrepreneurial general managers, a system which is known as 'leadership from the centre'. Managers are given considerable freedom in their managerial area, so long as they operate within the strategic and economic framework of the company. This freedom does not mean a scatter-gun approach, a tightly targeted 'corporate concept' guides employee actions, both setting standards and providing the freedom to create and see their efforts rewarded. This 'dynamic bureaucracy' offers a distinctive model for management and innovation.

---

decentralization to which he had been exposed to in the United States (where he was a prisoner of war). In many ways, in fact, Bertelsmann is some kind of bridge between thinking and sensing between continental Europe and the Anglo-Saxon world.

The personal influence of Reinhard Mohn has helped form the company into a wide range of medium-sized firms, each of which assumes for itself responsibility as well as business enterprise. This concept of social responsibility, which underpins Bertelsmann's relationship with society, has its counterpart in the idea of partnership which guides relations among employees. There is indeed a somewhat Japanese undertone to this aspect of Bertelsmann. According to this principle, employees should be treated as partners and be able to realize themselves as such through their work. One of the most visible manifestations of this partnership approach, in fact, is voluntary employee co-determination, embodied in the supervisory board. In the final analysis, all operations are guided by entrepreneurship, responsibility and partnership, perhaps straddling west, north and east. That is not a million miles away from the situation in Michelin in France.

Leading the World: Michelin and Salomon in France

The French are at home with large-scale enterprise in a way that is unique to Europe (perhaps excepting the Swedes). In that particular sense they have something in common with the Japanese. Michelin is a good case in point. In 1994, six companies across the globe were responsible for 80 per cent of the world's tyre production and sales. Michelin was the largest of these, with a market share of 20 per cent; Bridgestone of Japan came next with 18 per cent, and Goodyear of America was third with 15 per cent.

While Michelin has been described as a science and technology based company, its sales orientation is equally strong. At the same time its expenditures on R&D, as a percentage of turnover, significantly exceeds that of its competitors. Finally, and unusually in the world for such a large-scale enterprise, Michelin remains family owned and controlled.

A Family-based Enterprise

Michelin has been headed by François Michelin, the grandson of one of the company's founders, since 1955. One of his children, Edouard, a 32-year-old graduate of a leading French engineering school, appears destined to be the fourth generation head of the firm. Michelin, like several other French companies such as Yves St Laurent, is a public company with the status of 'SCA' (Société en Commandité par Action). As such, control rests with active family partners – 'commandités' – who are named in the company statutes and may vote for their own replacements, but cannot be forced to stand down by the shareholders. In that familial context there is a distinct touch of southern-ness – or 'feeling centred-ness', in Jung's terms – within the French Michelin context.

A Tradition of Employment and Innovation

Product innovation has been important throughout Michelin's history. The company invented the radial tyre in 1946, and in 1991 introduced a new 'green' tyre, described by the company as the most important innovation in the industry since the radial tyre. At the same time Michelin has tried to reduce any systematic relocation of manufacturing facilities in Asia or Eastern Europe in order to remain a significant employer in Clermont-Ferrand.

The company's strong corporate culture is thus not only attached externally to the region but also internally to its own employees. Michelin seeks out people who want a lifelong career in the company, and attempts to fit the job to the person, rather than vice versa. The rotation and training of personnel across functions and nations is part of an ongoing acculturation process, and the development of individual potential receives constant attention. François Michelin's conviction is that ideas are fragile and must be nurtured. Thus the company identifies creative individuals and offers them progressively enlarged responsibilities within project based activities. 'Researchers must have the resources and the freedom to experiment. One of them had the genius to try silica, even though 50 years ago the experiment had proved ineffective. That did not stop this man.' François Michelin himself spend a lot of time discussing and reviewing research in process, learning about new research hypotheses, and encouraging people.

Michelin: product and process innovation

Michelin, based in the industrial city of Clermont-Ferrand in central France, is one of the world's leading tyre manufacturers. In 1946 Michelin revolutionized the tyre market with the invention of the radial tyre, and it has continued to develop a series of new products over the years. In 1991 another radical innovation, the 'green' radial tyre, was introduced and has since made steady gains in the market.

As well as product innovation, Michelin has also placed much stress on process innovation. Under pressures from its competitors such as Pirelli and Bridgestone, which had made great strides towards innovation, Michelin set out to make a breakthrough in manufacturing. The result, in 1993, was the automation system C3M, which, installed in a new factory near Clermont-Ferrand, has improved flexibility and quality while simultaneously lowering costs.

Michelin is owned by the Michelin family, and François Michelin is the third generation of that family to lead the firm. He takes a strong personal interest in innovations, and supports innovation teams with time and resources. Innovations in Michelin can take a long time to develop – eleven years for C3M, seven for the green tyre – but Michelin believes this is a price worth paying to achieve radical innovation.

Energy Mobilized from the Top

In summary, nine aspects of corporate culture serve to facilitate innovation within Michelin:

- The largest budget in the industry is dedicated to R&D.
- The culture supports both science and technology and also commercial activities.
- Individuals with strong creative potential are identified early on in their careers, after which they are allocated progressively enlarged responsibilities.
- Space, time and resources are given to innovation.
- A blending of different international and scientific cultures facilitates variety.
- Special projects are isolated from the mainstream research activities, to enhance the possibility of making breakthroughs.

- Top management displays an active interest in the research process.
- The intense political commitment from the top to the strategic outcome of innovation mobilizes energy throughout the organization.
- The pursuit of a long-term vision is guaranteed by the continued family ownership and control.

The last point in particular is also the case with Salomon.

Establishing a 'Culte de Produit'

In forty years, Salomon has reached a position of world leadership in the field of alpine boots, alpine skis and Nordic boots and bindings, while also – more recently – becoming involved with the development and manufacture of golf clubs. The company is controlled by the Salomon family, who combine their Savoyard regional origins with a Jewish ethnic heritage. As such they have trading connections on two cultural counts. The resultant family control contributes to the stability of the social system in which the company is lodged. At the same time a competitive spirit is infused into all aspects of the company life, duly reinforced by the sporting world with which the company is so closely connected.

Salomon has developed what is termed a *culte du produit*, whereby innovation is centred upon a product concept over and above a technology or process. Accordingly, the company has evolved a differentiation strategy built upon product concepts and brands with unique characteristics, targeted at upper segments of the market. Because of the high value provided to customers, in terms of quality and design, performance and pleasure, the innovation process as a whole is a relatively slow one. Product development is essentially a cross-functional, cross-business activity. An adaptive, evolutionary organizational structure thereby facilitates the horizontal link between the prospective clients themselves, the development engineers, manufacturing departments and actual consumers. This

Salomon: the cult of the product

Salomon SA was founded in Savoy in 1947 by François and Jeanne Salomon and their son Georges as a maker of wooden ski blades and edges. Today, the firm has a turnover of nearly 4000 million francs. The firm remains a world leader in the manufacture of ski equipment, and top athletes such as the French downhill champion Carole Merle use Salomon skis. As well as ski equipment it has diversified into golf clubs and bicycles.

Throughout the company's history, Georges Salomon has played a leading role both as an innovator in his own right (in 1952 he designed an automatic opening binding which became one of the company's leading products) and as a driving force for innovation in the company. In the late 1980s after financial problems arose, the company recruited a management professional, Jean-François Gaultier, who is now president of the managing board, but Salomon still plays an active role in the company and his children also hold key posts in the firm. The family also own a large proportion of the company's stock.

Salomon is deeply rooted in the culture of Savoy, where there is a strong work ethic and sense of craftsmanship. The ethic at Salomon is one of seeking perfection in products, no matter how long it takes; the company would rather be second to the market than risk having the wrong product. This cult of the product infuses the entire company from Georges Salomon himself on down.

cultural orientation of the business towards interactivity fosters the interconnections between the potential needs of consumers, new product concepts and the possibilities offered by new technologies and processes.

Corporate proprietary knowledge related to new product development and marketing in the industry is formalized, protected, systematically updated and communicated to managers. As such, the overall corporate image has changed from one that is focused on leadership toward one that is oriented towards product design, innovation, quality and performance.

Salomon and Michelin can be seen to blend a number of characteristics. Their orientation towards individual creativity and product branding may be seen as 'western', similar to practices in attitudes in America. On the other hand their bureaucratic structures are distinctly European, more akin to Germany than American or even Britain. Their approach to quality and design is distinctly holistic, with similarities to Japanese approaches, while in their family-centredness they resemble firms in Italy and Spain.

Economic and Social Renewal: Mondragón and Banco de Santander in Spain

The first Spanish co-operatives appeared in the agricultural sector in the mid-nineteenth century. During the war many reached a significant size, but then had to be abandoned in Franco's Spain, when many of the leaders fled into exile once their assets were confiscated. In the Basque country, however, immediately after the war, a young priest named Father José Maria Arizmendiarrieta developed his own vision of a classless society, where education would be promoted through work. Inspired by the Christian tenet of the dignity of man, he maintained a deep commitment to the potential that resided within every person.

Continuous Education and Development

The founder's strong orientation towards education ultimately led the Mondragón Group to launch many an institution that was connected with the creation and diffusion of knowledge. Amongst these a Polytechnic Institute (Eskola Politeknikoa), a Management School (Eteo) and a Research Centre (Ikerlan) are the most prominent. In addition there are other institutes that provide technical training, together with one devoted specifically to the management of co-operatives and another serving as a new business incubator.

The new business incubator, Saiolan, also launched an Apprenticeship School, which is now funded by the regional government. According to one of Mondragón's founders, 'Saiolan plays the role Caja Laboral did in the past with its

Enterprise Division. Internal initiatives are channelled through the cluster level, rather than stand-alone new ventures being created.'

Co-operative Banking

Crucial to the success of what was to become the Mondragón Group of Basque co-operatives, and directly attributable to Father Jose Maria, was the creation of a financial arm to the business, the Caja Laboral Popular Bank, and, closely associated with it, Lagun-Aro, the pension fund of the group. One of the roles given to Caja Laboral Popular was that of helping to launch new co-operatives, that is those with a realistic business plan and appropriate leadership. With the explosion of demand in Spain throughout the 1960s the co-operative group expanded rapidly. However, after the energy crisis in the 1970s and the recession in the early 1980s a decision was taken to reorganize the group into three divisions: Capital Goods, Consumer Goods and Components. Within these divisions co-operatives were loosely organized in clusters. However, there has since been an attempt to link them all under the common brand image of Fangor.

In the 1990s a major organizational innovation ensued, representing a genuine transformation of the original Co-operative Congress. The Group in fact created a General Mondragón Board, representing an attempt to re-view the set of co-operatively based companies from the outside, rather than merely from within. Mondragón's bank and pension fund were thereby transformed into the financial division of the newly established corporation.

Fostering Independence and Interdependence

Mondragón is a unique phenomenon in the business world, a group of co-operative enterprises which have managed to sustain themselves as a socio-political as well as a techno-economic force. Ten features of their corporate culture stand out

Mondragón: a co-operative culture

The history of the Mondragón Co-operative Corporation begins with the arrival of a Catholic priest, Father José Maria Arizmendiarrieta, in the Basque town of Mondragón in 1941. In an effort to improve the economic lot of the local working-class families, Father José Maria began first by helping provide education through an industrial arts programme for boys and then, in 1956, setting up a workers' co-operative, known as Ulgor. From this simple beginning has come a network of co-operatives which in 1989 were grouped together under the Mondragón Co-operative Corporation. The group is now expanding its operations to other parts of Spain and to France.

The unique structure of Mondragón is a result of both its own corporate history and of the strongly self-deterministic and independent Basque culture. Pride, loyalty and industriousness are combined in equal measure. The paternalistic spirit of Father José Maria remains an important force, and many top managers are people who knew him well and have made his mission part of their own goals. At the same time the co-operative structure, where everyone is an owner, means that the co-operative has a responsibility to protect the worker.

R&D is carried out both by units within individual co-operatives and by separate co-operatives such as Ikerlan. Established in 1975, Ikerlan is charged with studying and creating new technologies with a ten-year time horizon. By creating Ikerlan as a distinct unit, equal yet separate within the group, Mondragón has ensured that these same values of self-determination and long-term vision that pervade the group are also built into its innovation strategies.

in that respect. First, ultimate control of the combined enterprises rests firmly and democratically with the general assembly of the entire workforce, albeit that recently external stakeholders have begun to play a more active role.

Second, each worker-member needs to purchase a significant stake in the enterprise, and this stake will rise or fall, depending on the fortunes of his or her enterprise. Third, a significant proportion of the group's capital is and remains collectively owned and indivisible, thereby enhancing the long term vision of Mondragón as a communal enterprise. Fourth, the initiative for the setting up of a new co-operative normally

Banco de Santander:
aggression, opportunism and speed to market

Founded in 1857, Banco de Santander remained a local bank until 1942, when it began to grow through acquisitions. In the 1950s it began to expand more rapidly in Spain, and also commenced operations in Latin America; by 1995 it had a presence in forty countries around the world. The architects of this growth were Emilio Botin and his father, successive presidents of the bank during the period of its greatest growth; the Botin family are also the bank's leading shareholders.

In Spain, Banco de Santander has a reputation as an aggressive and opportunistic firm. Its culture is typically Spanish, exemplifying virtues such as loyalty, austerity and low profile, but it combines these with individual values of aggressiveness and creativity displayed by its leaders. The banks employees are strongly loyal to both their firm and their leader, and are proud of working for one of the most successful firms in the country.

Banco de Santander has built its reputation on innovation and speed. It has been first into the market with many new financial products. When Spanish capital markets liberalized in the 1980s, Banco de Santander was first to react to the change and seize new market opportunities. In the words of one senior executive, innovation became a culture and a challenge, and that culture has led to the Bank's considerable economic success.

comes from a group of people, albeit that one of them may play a leadership role. It is a necessary condition, for support, that such a group has sufficient commitment to the undertaking. Fifth, wage and salary differentials, which today stand at a maximum of six to one, take account of the needs of group solidarity as well as market conditions.

Sixth, the separate executive functions of management are not only clearly defined, but such management, while appointed by and answerable to the membership, normally have security of tenure for four years. Seventh, isolated individual co-operatives have continuous access to a wide range of professional expertise, as well as to a continuous supply of newly skilled workers. Moreover, and eighth, the co-ops have continuous access to capital for expansion and to tide over hard times. At the same time, the co-operatives – partly though their backing for local educational and social projects – enjoy the support of the community. Finally, while the independence of each individual and co-operative enterprise is strongly guarded, their interdependence within the group is clearly in evidence.

Blending the Old with the New

Mondragón, over the course of the last fifty years, has had to continually adapt its old forms to new circumstances. Similarly the most successful of Spain's banking enterprises, Banco de Santander, although more conventional in business form, has had to make similar efforts to mix tradition with modernity. While management remains firmly entrenched within family hands, the young generation has concertedly opened up the development of the bank to professional managers from outside of the traditional banking domain. In that context traditional values of paternalism, loyalty and family respect have been combined with a more contemporary desire for self-determination as a professional operator in the individual's own right. It is this blend of old and new values, in effect, which have lain at the heart of the bank's innovative stance in recent years. This may in fact be Spain's contribution to European business. Along with Italy, Spain has blended together 'northern' modernity, via technology, with 'southern' tradition, via community.

Managing Diversity: Versace and Esaote in Italy

According to Esaote's founder, Carlo Castellano, five main elements serve to account for the company's success. The first two, he maintains, are particularly Italian. These are accounted for by the state-backed corporate sector, to which his company belonged for twelve years, and the publicly funded research system, which helped Esaote to develop the knowledge base it needed to compete. Three further factors are specific to Esaote as opposed being general for Italy. These consist firstly of the company's low-profile strategy, whereby it wanted to show Italian industrialists that it was able to create a real business enterprise rather than a mere research laboratory. Secondly, Esaote set out to accommodate a degree of cultural diversity within the business, particularly with respect to the Genoan and Florentine regions in which the company was respectively based. Finally, Esaote had brought together a highly cohesive and yet diverse management team.

The Esaote product range in fact, upon which the company is based, extends from magnetic resonance imaging to ultrasound to an artificial pancreas. The core product is ultrasound, an easily manoeuvrable diagnostic tool, based upon the reflection of high frequency sounds, geared towards the identification of the inner workings of specifically differentiated parts of the body. The range of ownership has historically extended from public to private enterprise, recently emerging through a management buy-out, involving the bulk of Esaote's personnel.

Creation, Orientation and Elaboration

Esaote has passed through many phases in its thirteen-year history. It began as a start-up inside the state-owned Finmec-canica group, as a division of Ansaldo (Genova), based on the commercialization of Hitachi products and development of an internal knowledge base. At this stage the company was very much in the state sector culture, and its attributes were largely those of its locale in Genoa. The focus was internal and knowledge-specific, and the emphasis was on creation.

The next, developmental phase focused on the development of an industrial core as Esaote strove to find its own place and cut ties with its state-owned parent. The key activity in this stage was the acquisition of (and merger with) the Florentine company Ote Biomedica, which had core strengths in this

Esaote: building on a knowledge base

Esaote Biomedica was established in 1981 as Esacontrol, as part of the Italian state-owned company Ansaldo-Finmeccanica (the name was changed when Esacontrol acquired the Florentine firm Ote Biomedica in 1986). The firm's primary products are medical imaging equipment such as ultrasound and magnetic resonance imaging (MRI) scanners. Turnover in 1994 was 233 billion lira, or approximately $145 million. In July 1994 the company's managers bought the company into the private sector through a management buy-out.

The founder, Carlo Castellano, had been head of strategic planning with Ansaldo; he was also a communist. His fellow managers of the new firm were primarily engineers and technicians. The genesis of the firm lay in Castellano's personal interest in medical imaging equipment and view that there was a market opportunity ready to be exploited. Although the new company had little backing from its parent and virtually no working capital it had, as Castellano readily appreciated, a very strong knowledge base. In the early days of the company the emphasis was almost entirely on R&D, working with foreign partners such as Hitachi to bring products to market. The company's strength, then as now, was the combination of diversity of ideas and backgrounds and cohesion of thought and practice, particularly among the top management team.

With growth, particularly the acquisition of Ote, the company moved into production of its own product lines. The owner-managers now feel that Esaote is a European rather than Italian company, and they are preparing to launch it into the world market. They are acutely conscious of the firm's national and intra-national heritage; the acquisition of Ote added an 'Umbrian' aspect to the firm's Genoese culture, and the harmonizing of these two cultures is considered a source of strength. What the company's managers fear now is losing their unique Italian heritage under the pressures of the global market.

sector and had already developed a flexible network of suppliers in the Tuscan region. The melding of Genoese and Tuscan/Umbrian cultures helped Esaote become more distinctly Italian and added core strengths during this orientation phase.

Finally, there have been two elaboration phases. The first was internationalization, which saw Esaote create commercial companies in Germany and France and acquire an American

---

Versace: vehicle for a talent

The fashion house Gianni Versace SpA was founded in Milan in 1978.
It has since become one of the largest and most respected fashion houses
in the world; its designs have won numerous awards and have
appeared in films and on stage as well as on all the world's major
catwalks. In 1994, group sales totalled $650 million world-wide.

The company exists as a vehicle for the creative genius of Gianni
Versace, who is the company's leading creative talent. His brother
Santo, the group managing director, and other family members take
charge of the process whereby Gianni's creative concepts are produced
and marketed. The talents of the supreme innovator are exploited
efficiently by people who are close to him, while Gianni himself is to
some extent isolated from the day to day pressures of the market and
is free to devote himself to creative work.

In the Versace group, the strong interdependence between family
members with diverse interests plays a key role in supporting
innovation. In a company which spans the entire range between
technology and art, this mix of diversity and dependence has played a
crucial role in corporate and personal success.

---

distributor. The second was privatization, with the whole
company – management and employees – investing in a buyout
to take the company into the private sector. From its local and
national bases, Esaote is now moving into European and world
spheres, a move which Castellano knows will have significant
effects on corporate culture.

Elaboration Through the Family

While Esaote is led by a tight-knit management team from
diverse backgrounds, Versace is an example of a family-based
firm of a type which Italy has known for centuries. Versace's
success as a firm has rested on two pillars: the creative genius
of Gianni Versace himself, and the family support provided by
his brother Santo and sister Donatella, who together with
Gianni make up the triumvirate at the top of the company.

Again we can see the progression through the three stages,
but this time with the family as the prime vehicle. The first

stage, creation, was led by Gianni Versace himself, who moved from Calabria to Milan to establish himself as a designer. The second stage, orientation, came with the transformation of the company from a design agency to a producer, not only of clothing but also of accessories, textiles, watches, jewellery, perfumes and furniture; it was at this stage that Santo joined the firm, adding management strength to design strength. The third stage, elaboration, can be seen in the steady internationalization and expansion that has led first to a range of strong relationships with external clients and then to the opening of wholly-owned shops and boutiques around the world.

The strong relationships inside the Versace family have been transferred to the firm; indeed, it is impossible to explain the evolution of Versace as a firm without understanding the role of the family. The management provided by his brother and sister give Gianni Versace complete freedom to work on the creative side and pursue his own vision. Cultural excellence and economic success have thus gone hand in hand.

Chapter 8

- -

Capturing the Universal Principles of Innovation

Notwithstanding the diversity of the thirteen companies, there are underlying similarities in the way in which they support innovation. These we have captured as the universal principles of innovation, of which we find ten.

We can additionally use the concepts of *knowledge, vision* and *commercialization* as a framework with which to structure these ten principles. Where a principle supports more than one of the three concepts, it has been placed where it contributes the most.

- Information: the explicit use of information sharing mechanisms (see p. 80).
- Linked basic competencies (see p. 83).

Information sharing mechanisms and linked basic competencies are key elements in the **knowledge** creation process.

- Leadership: the presence of a founder or CEO with a clear vision of innovation (see p. 85).
- Commitment to innovation shared by all members of the firm (see p. 89).

Knowledge	Vision	Commercialization
• Information	• Leadership	• Market awareness
• Linked competencies	• Commitment	• Organization
	• Strategy	• Resources
	• Regeneration	• Incentivization

Figure 8.1 Key success factors

- Strategy: a long-term approach to management and a basis of stability (see p. 91).
- Regeneration: a willingness to start all over again (see p. 95).

Leadership and commitment to innovation, the long-term view but at the same time the willingness to question past positions in favour of new solutions all form part of the **visionary** character of a company.

- Market awareness: the distance between innovation and the market (see p. 97).
- Organization: the use of flat organizational structures and teamwork (see p. 99).
- Resources: the allocation of resources to support innovation (see p. 104).
- Incentivization: a reward structure that supports innovative behaviour (see p. 109).

These last four principles are all critical in the commercialization process within the above framework. The ten universal principles of innovation are elaborated upon in the following text.

Information: The Explicit Use of Information Sharing Mechanisms

Adopting an organizational structure that subdivides the organization and encourages responsibility in small units is useful, but runs the risk of fragmentation. Without some binding mechanisms in place, a firm may break into many small units and lose the ability to share information or leverage its scope and scale. Not surprisingly, therefore, most of the firms in the study relied intensively on mechanisms to share information, partly for purposes of control but more importantly to facilitate communication and share knowledge among units.

Strong internal mechanisms for knowledge creation are unsurprisingly present in Japanese firms such as Kao and Sharp, which are exemplars of knowledge creating and sharing organizations. Kao, for instance, identifies among its 'enabling conditions' the use of flexible project teams, frequent personnel rotation and systems of information sharing. More intriguing was to find that many European firms make similar efforts. Mondragón, for instance, has an explicit policy of managerial rotation, and Psion uses interdisciplinary teams throughout its organization for everything from procurement to sales. Both of these firms are explicit in their efforts to share information within the firm.

Trumpf uses a variety of communications channels (regular, informal and formal, at all levels, across levels, on-site and off-site), 'horizontal loops' as co-ordinating mechanisms, the Trumpf Optimization Program (TOP) for continuous improvement in R&D and the use of production units which cut across organizational units to overcome problems of decentralization. The establishment and maintenance of effective communication networks is very strongly emphasized; these networks not only serve as a means to detect what is currently going on in the internal and external environment, but also to allow the sharing of hard-won technical knowledge. In order to foster extensive information on the part of all employees, Trumpf uses a broad array of measures including:

- monthly person-to-person co-ordination talks at all hierarchical levels
- management conferences (four times a year)
- shop-floor meetings
- management information letters
- a company newspaper for all employees ('Trumpf Aktuell')
- monthly information of all employees in production facilities
- at least one quarterly visit by executives to subsidiaries
- three-day meetings of international managers once a year
- weekly meetings of heads of central departments
- strategy weekends
- conferences of plant managers, quality managers and service managers
- interdisciplinary teams
- an open-door principle
- close contact with top management (for example, informal 'fireside talks' with Dr Leibinger, the CEO)

Besides these measures, Trumpf supports personal, informal networks between employees in different departments. Taken together, all these measures do not only foster a good information on the part of employees. They are also important measures to reinforce the corporate culture.

The flat structure of Mondragón, the concentration of management and employees in the narrow valley of Mondragón itself and the social traditions of the Basque community all facilitate horizontal communications across companies, functions and layers. The austere compensation system makes possible shifts in the organization related to the fit of the person in a given place and given a moment in time, without all the typically complex factors of promotion, compensation and career. The internal bureaucracy of Mondragón, which requires a high level of consensus, also requires good communication. Mondragón is a transparent organization, and information is accessible at all levels. Specific systems such as the 'technology inventory' and the 'design guideline' distribute and share technological information inside the group. Salomon and Bertelsmann have also developed good internal communication flows; at the top level, the latter uses a novel board structure with interlocking directorates. World management congresses are used as a means to improve co-operation among the profit centres, to provide information about overall strategic direction and the corporate framework of business operations, and to enforce corporate culture as well as the corporate identity. Close informational connections are enhanced by a high degree of personal communications and a low degree of formalization.

Similarly, communications are seen as very important at Microsoft. Nearly all of the firm's employees (12,000 in 1994) are located at the Microsoft 'campus' on a large tract of wooded land in Redmond, Washington, ten miles east of Seattle. Over the years, although growing at a remarkable rate and adding many new employees, Microsoft has tried to retain the feel of a small firm. Many employees cited the extensive use of electronic mail as an important element of direct and open communication; employees can and do use e-mail to communicate directly with Bill Gates and other managers on a variety of issues, and typically received answers quickly and personally.

Linked Basic Competencies

We will less discuss the need for having a set of basic competencies, related in such a way that they can be combined in differing configurations such that many innovations can be spawned: this is well understood in principle, though perhaps less well executed in practice, particularly by some larger European companies. What we will discuss is how to obtain these competencies, in particular through acquisition or alliance. The reason for this focus is that acquisitions or alliances, except in the case of simply acquiring the rights to a new technology, introduces a new culture into the company.

Not all innovations can be developed internally, and practically all the European companies studied engaged in alliances to boost their innovative capacity. Internal R&D efforts tended to be focused on carefully selected areas that were considered to be in the companies' core competency or most differentiating domain. Medium to long term relationships were then established with other companies which had the ability to make contributions which enhanced these core areas. In some cases, the alliance became an acquisition because the company acquired was also working in these core areas, or because the buyer had decided to enter into a new business and the acquired company would provide a good basis for growth.

Trumpf, for example, acquired Haas Laser in order to strengthen its laser capabilities. In order to keep its leading position in the area of research, Trumpf engages also in co-operative arrangements with universities (especially with the technical universities in Stuttgart, Aachen and Munich) and other research facilities such as the Fraunhofer Institut. In the past Trumpf has also co-operated with various firms in order to develop new products. Those co-operative arrangements were, however, not very successful; Trumpf management feels that the company has more know-how than its partners and that Trumpf could do the job faster and more efficiently.

Mondragón has engaged in many alliances with European and Japanese companies, such as an alliance with Hitachi in the development of freezers or with Thomson in the development of commercial alliances. Mondragón has also begun an ambitious process of acquisitions. Bertelsmann has focused on acquisitions in areas where it has product-related core-competencies. Apparently some organizational learning took place with regard to the focus on core competencies; in the 1970s, for example, Bertelsmann's acquisitions included a software firm and a huge chicken farm. Neither acquisition was successful and both were divested. Looking at Bertelsmann's acquisition strategy, a saw-tooth pattern emerges; periods of major acquisitions are usually followed by periods of internal growth where the primary task is the consolidation of acquired operations.

In its management of acquisitions, Bertelsmann aims at maintaining and not destroying creativity and innovativeness. It does not try to impose a certain media vision but instead allows subsidiaries the autonomy to apply previous experience and develop new ideas. The Bertelsmann approach to decentralization suggests that allowing for entrepreneurial freedom while at the same time providing management support is a key factor of success in the management of acquisitions.

The Italian firm Esaote has also a considerable activity in terms of alliances and acquisitions; in 1982 it signed a contract with Hitachi for the development of an ultrasound imaging diagnostics machine, and in 1986 it acquired Ote Biomedical. Silica (the basis for Michelin's green tyre) was developed by French chemical giant Rhone Poulenc, which now supplies Michelin operations around the world. Salomon subcontracts those activities that are not part of its core competencies; the production of its top product, the monocoque ski, is integrated close to the company's headquarters in Annecy, but more standard skis are produced, for example, by Blizzard, an Austrian independent manufacturer. Dolomite, a company established in Montebelluna, Italy, works with Salomon in the development of new products, and ski shoes are subcontracted to manufacturers in Italy and Romania. Salomon has also acquired new core competencies by buying companies which manufacture golf clubs and bicycles.

Leadership: The Presence of a Founder or CEO with a Clear Vision of Innovation

A painting begins as a vision in the mind of the artist. An innovation begins as a vision in the mind of a manager or entrepreneur. Successful innovations are those which begin the mind of someone who has the power to fulfil them. In most cases, this means that 'someone' has to be at or near the top of the organization, and in most of the cases studied, this meant the founder or the CEO. Consistently, as already indicated in Chapter 5, it appeared that the presence of a CEO with a clear vision and who could act as a source of inspiration and a catalyst for action was vitally important. Quite simply, this person acts as a personification of the spirit of innovation within the firm.

In many of the firms studied, the founder remains as the guiding light of innovation: Carlo Castellano at Esaote, David Potter at Psion, George Salomon at Salomon, Bill Gates at Microsoft, Gianni Versace at Versace. In others, notably Sharp and Mondragón, although the founder is no longer with the firm, that person still represents a tangible commitment to forward thinking and innovation. Often, as in the case of Dr Berthold Leibinger at Trumpf, the CEO has strong technical competence and can set a personal example in guiding the innovative processes of the firm, and again it is notable that many of the corporate leaders surveyed here – Gianni Versace, Georges Salomon, Bill Gates, David Potter – were personally responsible for early and successful innovations.

Where top managers are not themselves directly responsible for innovation, they are nonetheless responsible for setting the pace of innovation within the company. In all the companies surveyed, not only was the priority given by top management to innovation very high, but the corporate leaders were also sending out a very explicit message to every employee to the effect that innovation transcended all aspects of the corporate life. Many of the top managers of the companies surveyed devoted a very large proportion of their time to innovation; Bill Gates divides his time equally between R&D and marketing, and at Trumpf, direct responsibility for innovation rests with the company's number two, the vice-president. In many of these cases the image of the company is closely linked to the image of the top manager, who often is also one of the leading shareholders.

In most instances, the most important aspect of the personal image these people have chosen to project is that of 'successful innovator' rather than 'successful businessman'. In David Potter, for example, one can see an almost romantic attitude to innovation, discovery and learning which at times still transcends the requirements of business.

Top Management Orientation Towards Innovation

In most innovative companies around the world, innovation will appear high in the ranking of the top management priorities; it is likely that even in companies that do not show an outstanding record of innovation, top management would assign great importance to this function. In the thirteen companies studied, priority given by the top management to innovation was both very high and very high-profile.

In Europe, the most immediately obvious feature was the close personal relationship between leaders and innovation. Not only did leaders put innovation at the top of their agenda, but people such as François Michelin of Michelin, David Potter of Psion and Javier Mongelos of Mondragón all had a clear personal bias towards and interest in innovation. Anyone looking at their firms' annual report, reading company magazines or listening to their speeches at important corporate events could be left in no doubt of this. Over at Trumpf, both Dr Berthold Leibinger, the CEO, and vice-chairman Hans Klingel take direct responsibility for innovation. The high level of involvement, coupled with a high level of technological expertise at the very top, has led to the formulation of a technology vision which guides the evolution of technological core competencies.

These and other top managers in the firms studied spend much of their time on innovation. As noted in the previous chapter, these firms also tend to spend more than average on R&D, with the impetus again coming from the top.

Of course there is nothing exclusively European about this attitude, and in the USA Microsoft in particular shares many of the same values. But there are nonetheless some distinctively European values and attitudes held by the nine European companies in the survey. For example, constant day-to-day involvement by very senior managers (including the CEO) in the innovation process is something that is much more common in Europe than in Japan and the United States, where responsibility for innovation is pushed much further down the hierarchy and out into the business units and teams. Let us look first at an American approach. At Microsoft, Bill Gates assumes a central role in co-ordinating the efforts of development teams:

> If I see that a group is having unexpected difficulties or is moving slowly, I might assign a 14 [a high-ranking software architect; six top software architects, possessing the highest ranking of Level 15, report directly to Gates] to join the group, determine the problem and help out.

At other times Gates intercedes directly in discussions among various development teams whose efforts are interdependent. Gates' approach is to say to each: 'Don't worry about the others; I will guarantee that they deliver their product with the right specifications at the right time. You just develop your piece and don't worry about the rest.' In this way the various teams can work simultaneously rather than sequentially, speeding up the development process and avoiding the friction of having to negotiate with each other.

The difference is subtle in appearance but important in practice. Although as noted above, Gates and his top managers are responsible for much of the concept development at Microsoft, once responsibility for development has been assigned, the creative work is done by the project teams. Gates' role is to coordinate and adjudicate disputes, not to command and control. Responsibility for innovation rests with the teams, not with Gates.

This is not a question of hierarchical management, but of *hierarchy of innovation*. At Psion, a flat-structured company which makes great use of teams, innovation cascades down through the company, from vision at the top to materialization at the lower levels. The technologically based vision and evolving market context is primarily provided by the founder and CEO, David Potter. Potter usually has the creative idea – he is good also at putting himself in the customer's shoes – and the development people are good at materialization. Potter has the ability to plant in the development team's minds a real vision, and then motivate them to take it forward.

At Trumpf, as mentioned above, responsibility and very often day to day control rests with the top managers, even the CEO. In this way it is guaranteed that inventions do not get lost within the organization; rather, the intense involvement by top management in innovation allows the rapid exploitation of new developments. Salomon, Mondragón and Versace are other examples of firms where the CEO remains the guiding spirit of innovation within the company. Even in highly decentralized Bertelsmann, managers of business units are actively involved in innovation (which in this case means the creation of new business rather than the creation of new products) and innovation is a major priority of top management.

These distinctive European managerial attitudes towards innovation manifest themselves in a variety of ways, which are reflected in corporate organization and culture (as will be discussed further below). First, the central concepts of continuity and long term innovation are enhanced by physically placing the innovation function in a location close to corporate headquarters and in the region where the corporation was born (noticeable especially at Michelin, Mondragón and Trumpf). Second, there is a deliberate strategy of creating a peculiar, distinctive and protected, almost paternalistic, way to innovate (seen especially at Trumpf, Michelin, Salomon and Versace). Third, there is a special prestige, or elitism (a sense of being separated from the crowd) for those directly involved in the innovation process (seen at Michelin, Salomon and Esaote). Finally, as noted above, there is an apparent preference on the part of European leaders for being perceived by society as technicians and successful innovators rather than financially successful businessmen.

Commitment to Innovation

Beyond specific mechanisms, a common feature in many innovative firms was a broad and deep commitment to innovation by all members of the firm. Rather than viewing innovation as somehow the responsibility of a few employees, such as members of the R&D department, most or all employees came to view innovation as their personal responsibility.

One of the best examples of this attitude comes from Raychem, a firm outside this study but whose founder Paul Cook is worth quoting:

> There's no one in any organization who can't be clever and imaginative about doing his or her job more effectively. We expect innovation from our secretaries and the people on the loading docks as well as from the scientists.

Many American firms constantly communicate to all their employees the importance of developing new products as a source of continuing revenues. This view of innovation as something systemic which permeates the organization can be found in Japanese and European firms as well. Japanese firms, with their belief in *kaizen* or continuous improvement, have made such an approach an integral part of their organizations. In Europe, Mondragón has a culture of improvement based on an explicit emphasis on training and continuous improvement; at Psion, an attitude permeates the firm wherein 'creativity and play is not considered to be inconsistent with serious planning.'

The systemic nature of innovation was perhaps best seen at Banco de Santander, where profitable innovation was viewed as 'an explicit objective'. In the words of the bank's COO:

Innovation became a culture and a challenge; everybody must innovate; innovation becomes a critical element of the dynamics of the bank, a form of internal competition. Of course, there has to be a certain tolerance for failure if you want to create a learning organization, although with the sin you get the punishment.

Strategy: A Long-term Approach to Management and a Basis of Stability

Another key similarity between the firms studied is an explicit long-term approach towards management, emphasizing concepts such as stable employment and promotion from within. The existence of such policies at Kao and Sharp is not surprising, as Japanese firms have long been known for their policies of lifetime employment. It is, however, somewhat more remarkable that in their analyses of European firms such as Salomon, Michelin, Banco Santander and Trumpf, researchers noted an explicit emphasis on long-term employment, promotion from within and overall stability. Examples of emphasis on long-term stability can also be found in US firms such as Hewlett-Packard and 3M (not directly included in the study), suggesting a broad similarity among successful innovative firms.

The importance of a long-term attitude and the value of stability may not be immediately apparent. After all, innovation implies change; stability can lead to complacency, which is antithetical to change. Taking this view, embracing innovation may be difficult in an environment which prizes stability. However, it can be argued that a commitment to stability is important for employees, who are more likely to promote change if they do not feel threatened by it. When employees fear that changes will result in disruptions or even loss of employment, they may have little confidence in suggesting changes and in extreme cases may even try to block or prevent changes. Thus, providing a stable environment is far from the enemy of innovation; rather, it contributes to employee confidence and security, which may be vital in achieving innovation.

A long-term commitment is also vital for long-term planning, particularly in areas where a single project can take years to move from concept to market. Planning for innovation is another hallmark of the companies in the study. David Potter of Psion, a believer in creativity and play, is also a strong believer in planning:

> Development people need to create, but not in a vacuum. In fact, they are much happier working within a framework. Planning is not inconsistent with creativity. Organizer II is a development concept that was launched in the exact week we planned it to occur. There was good planning and organization throughout.

Trumpf implemented two major development programmes in the 1990s to improve overall efficiency, the Program for Potentials to Improve Results and, building on the success of this first programme, the Trumpf Optimization Program (TOP). TOP was initiated by Trumpf's top management with the goal of providing ways to build upon the competence, knowledge and ideas of all employees. TOP was described as 'a programme geared to optimize innovation processes and continuous improvement processes by changes of the behaviour of Trumpf employees in order to secure long-term company success on the grounds of the company's objectives'.

Salomon perceives itself as a slow-moving innovator; sometimes it is less important to be first in the market than it is to make a strong impact on the market. The new Salomon ski boot and the monocoque ski were both five years in development. Slowness is the price of maturation from the creative spark that initiates the process. A similar climate surrounds the major innovations of Michelin; it took eleven years to develop the C3M technology and seven years for the 'green tyre' and François Michelin personally spent many hours discussing projects with team leaders, reviewing research progress, learning about new hypotheses and difficulties and generally encouraging people. Planning is also high on the agenda at Microsoft, where innovation lies at the heart of the firm's competitive strategy. As mentioned above, Bill Gates spends half his time managing new product development; he and his team start with an idea for a new product, what it should do and when it should be released, and then work backwards to determine the level of staffing and other resources required.

The success of Banco de Santander as an innovator is to a great extent associated to its ability using time-to-market approaches in a market where rapid response and change is required. Time-to-market is also a crucial element of corporate strategy in Japan, where companies such as Sharp use a 'hypertext organization' to help shorten the innovation cycle. A hypertext organizational structure enables an organization to create and accumulate knowledge efficiently and effectively by transforming knowledge between two structural layers: the business system, which is organized as a traditional hierarchy, and the project team, which is organized as a typical task force. The knowledge generated in the two layers is then recategorized and recontextualized in the third layer, the knowledge layer.

The top management obsession with innovation is transformed into a well-defined strategy that places innovation at the centre of the business, and shapes other aspects of the business in order to produce a balanced approach to managing the corporation. At Bertelsmann, refinement of systems to co-ordinate very autonomous units is used to protect the 'sacrosanct' philosophy of decentralization and intrapreneurship, while at the same time building synergy and providing the autonomous units with the resources and other benefits of the large corporation. At Salomon, innovation-centred diversification to compensate for the seasonal character of winter sports-related products combines a focus on core competencies, outsourcing and rationalization to remain cost competitive in low growth markets. At Michelin, product and process innovations allow the company to lead in terms of product features and performance, while maintaining a flexible and lean production organization that makes it possible to compete in industrial countries from manufacturing locations in those countries. At Mondragón, internationalization and innovation have become the critical components of strategy; at Trumpf also, internationalization and innovation together are the core elements of corporate strategy. Manufacturing and distribution operations abroad reinforce the process of innovation; for example, Trumpf's establishment in the US and Japanese markets was undertaken with the aim of gaining understanding of customer needs and technology in those markets.

In all the European companies studied, innovation is a central element of a well-balanced strategy, in which everything spins around innovation and strengthens it. Innovation, for these companies, plays the same role that excellent marketing does for the corporate strategy of Coca-Cola, Unilever, Procter and Gamble or Sarah Lee, that world-class manufacturing does for Toyota, or that financial expertise does for Pearson or the March Group. European innovators build their strategies around innovation; everything else stems from it, and in turn affects it.

It should not necessarily be concluded that this bias towards innovation is a peculiarly European feature. Rather, the answer is that they organize themselves towards this strategy in a ways which fit their own local cultures, and that this itself is peculiarly European. The difference lies not in the elements of the strategy but in the ways in which strategy is controlled and driven, and here again we see the emphasis on control and direction from the very top. Trumpf, for example, is peculiar in that its seven top managers share among themselves the supervision and control of horizontal (functions) and vertical (business units) relationships. Salomon adapts its organization in order to create the conditions that better favour its competitive strategy and to increase the speed of innovation; from a typical geographic/product division structure, the company evolves to a product division structure and finally to an organization capable of deepening into the needs of customers while managing a creative tension. The organization becomes a critical element to facilitate the development of 'cult products'.

Mondragón has undergone a profound metamorphosis in order to preserve its co-operative identity, its autonomy at the base and its rooting in the Valley of Mondragón, while being able at the same time to respond to the competitive challenges of globalization with the conventional approaches of acquisitions, foreign investments and alliances. In other words, the company creates the mechanisms to preserve its own traditional culture while dealing also with any other culture. The core of Mondragón will continue to be a group of co-operatives, but a newly acquired company or a foreign investment will not need to be a co-operative as well.

In this respect Mondragón is a very Spanish company; indeed, it could be said that it is a Basque company. Trumpf in this same respect could be said to be very German. The conclusion is that European companies are capable of adopting innovation-biased strategies that, while having the same focus, are at the same time heavily adapted to fit corporate and environmental cultures.

Regeneration: A Willingness to Start All Over Again

Closely linked to the top management obsession with innovation is a vision of innovation which places at least some emphasis on breakthrough or conceptual innovation. For many of the companies studied, breakthrough innovation is a major ongoing goal; constant incremental innovation updates existing products, while breakthrough innovation reaches out to search for new products. It is the vision of top management which supports the drive for breakthrough innovation.

At Trumpf, for example, 81% of the products are younger than three years, and only 1% of the entire product range is older than six years. Focusing R&D activities on laser technologies and the acquisition of a new subsidiary, Haas Laser, has allowed for a continuous expansion of the range of products using this technology. Today Trumpf must be considered an industry leader in the field of machine tools based on laser technology.

The vision at Salomon is of 'changing the rules of the game' and developing 'cult products'. Changing the rules of the game means creating new concepts of products that frequently require a change in sporting practice by consumers, which in turn literally lead to a change of the rules of the game or technical standards in the industry. Developing 'cult products' means launching products with universal impact beyond cultures and ages. At Salomon they mention examples to define what they mean by 'cult products': the Sony Walkman, the Nike Air shoe, the Big Bertha golf club of Callaway, the Tour Preferred iron golf club of Taylor Made, and Salomon's own monocoque ski and SX91 alpine boot. When Georges Salomon decided to change the rules of the game in the world of the ski, he hired an R&D manager, Maurice Legrand, former R&D chief at Rossignol, and asked him to produce 'a ski completely different from any other existing ski'. The manager recalled later that 'Salomon bet everything on development. We were a small team and the boss came every day to meet us in our office. We had a very high motivation.'

Conceptual innovation has been a source of competitive advantage at Michelin all through the company's history. The company invented the radial tyre in 1946 which gave it a strong competitive edge. In 1991 Michelin introduced the new "green tyre" technology or green X that is described by the company as the most important breakthrough since the development of the radial tyre. The new product (called Energy in Europe, MXV4 in America and MXGS in Asia) offers significantly less rolling resistance than conventional tires and reduces fuel consumption by 5–6% without giving up any other performance characteristics. According to François Michelin, the creative individual has the capacity to face with an open mind the inadequacy of a conventional product to consumers' expectations or industrial needs. The essential quality is the capacity of the researcher to listen, to collect facts, to abandon preconceived ideas with a special blend of curiosity, admiration or questioning, a 'capacité d'emerveillement'.

At Mondragón, the corporate focus is on incremental innovation. However, there are areas where the corporation identifies the possibility of leading internationally with front of the line products. In these areas, the vision is formulated through the 'Project Guide' concept. The Project Guide is a futuristic definition of where the corporation wants to be with one line of products in the years to come. It is a kind of ambitious forecast of what the market will be expecting in the future of a specific product.

Not surprisingly, perhaps, the differences between European companies and their American and Japanese counterparts are here more subtle. Firms in the USA also show a strong willingness to pursue a vision of how their products should evolve, even at the expense of their current products. Successful innovators in America seem to have an accurate sense of opportunity for introducing new products. More interesting is that some of these firms demonstrate a willingness to cannibalize their current line of products in order to develop the next generation of products; rather than protecting their existing product line or milking it for as much profit as possible, they not only accept but even embrace change.

The Japanese innovators studied also had the ability to formulate a guiding vision for the development of their products. At Kao, the creative process is framed within a vision defining the knowledge domain of 'surface science'. This definition enabled the company, whose origin was in surface-active agents used in detergents, to move into new markets such as cosmetics and floppy disks. A skin cream can be looked at from a surface-science point of view as the surface between oil and skin, and a floppy disk as a plastic film coated with magnet powder. At Sharp, the core technology is 'opto-electronics', which represents the image of the world Sharp wants to live in, and is one of the key concepts describing what Sharp ought to be. The essence of Sharp's strategy based on opto-electronics could be described as a dynamic conversion of component technologies and product concepts.

Distance between Innovation and the Market

François Michelin expressed what might be considered as the European approach to the role of the market:

> At Michelin marketing and innovation go together: in order to innovate, researchers need continuous feedback on market conditions . . . scientists and engineers are true marketers.

It is in the last part of this comment that true significance lies. While European companies are no less aware of the need to produce innovations which will have a significant impact on the market than their American and Japanese counterparts, they have a somewhat different way of managing the relationship. Particularly for those firms where there is a strong commitment to breakthrough innovation, new products in Europe tend to be conceived at a distance from the market, out of a conceptual exercise, and then tested in the market. The market is used more as a feedback support to development than as an original stimulus for conceptualization.

The trait of Japanese companies, defined by Nonaka and Takeuchi (1995) as 'constructing a knowledge network with the outside world' seems to be less prominent in European companies, at least in those analysed in this study. In a knowledge network, rather than asking customers explicitly what they want, companies form a direct two-way communication with customers, using continual dialogue with and insight from customers to develop products. In European companies, this tends to happen only after the original product concept has been developed and is then being tested and refined. Once this stage has been reached, then market feedback plays a major role. Salomon used the French ski champion Carole Merle as a consultant on the monocoque ski project, and Merle herself describes the process:

> I work directly with the development office. I have tested hundreds of skis going over different types of snow, and little by little we have improved the performance. My technician was with me all the year round. He was the connection between the development office and me. I had sensations but he translated them into data that could be used by researchers.

This kind of attention to detail led athletes using Salomon products to win 37 gold medals in the Olympic Games in Lillehammer, Norway. Customers, in this case professional athletes, are also important in marketing plans, and Salomon spent a figure equivalent to 2% of its sales on marketing at Lillehammer. However, this should not obscure the fact that the original drive to produce the ski came from Georges Salomon, whose vision it was to develop a new ski that would dominate the market.

Another example of a European type of relationship between innovation and marketing can again be seen in Salomon, which in 1994 created the new position of project managers. The most important function expected from these managers is the strengthening of the co-ordination between development, market and resources. The new development machine at Salomon consists of the product managers helped by a management controller and three committees: strategy (connecting market and industrial studies), projects (connecting market study projects and industrial projects) and budgets. At other companies such as Bertelsmann, Psion, Versace and Esaote it is the entrepreneur who makes the synthesis between customer needs and development, which in the latter three companies in particular means the top managers (David Potter, Gianni Versace and Carlo Castellano). Usually it is one person who makes the decision, on the basis of a combination of experience, foresight, risk taking capability and knowledge of the business.

Organization: The Use of Flat Organizational Structures and Teamwork

The Sharp example shows the importance not only of planning but also of structure. Sharp uses the advantages of both hierarchy and flexible cross-functional teams. Virtually every one of the firms in the study addressed the organizational dimension of innovation. Firm after firm stressed the importance of flat organizations, with minimal hierarchical distinctions and few layers of bureaucracy. By flattening their organizations, communication between senior management and the front lines was swifter and bureaucratic procedures that can impede innovation were minimized.

Rather than add layers and extend the organization upwards, these firms tended to subdivide and extend laterally, using small groups as a key organizing principle. Most firms stressed the importance of small organizational units for innovation. American firms were particularly notable in this regard; Microsoft, for example, has a policy if subdividing business units once they become too large. There was a firm belief among managers of all the firms surveyed that, in terms of individual creativity, small units are considerably more effective than large ones.

The belief in flat organizational structures was explicit in the US and Japanese firms studied, IBM, Microsoft, Kao and Sharp, an unsurprising finding given recent trends in organization in the United States and Japan. More notable was the discovery that virtually all the European firms studied also espoused a belief in flat structures and the subdivision of units. Michelin, a large industrial firm that might have expected to exhibit a bureaucratic structure, relied on small teams which were given time, resources and independence from established core R&D units. Bertelsmann had a highly decentralized structure with more than 300 business units, each able to pursue its objectives with minimal control from the centre. Mondragón, was described as having a 'flat organization' with innovation managed in clusters; Trumpf took steps in the early 1990s to increase the decentralization of responsibility and to improve transparency through a simplified manufacturing structure. Trumpf also actively used 'management by projects' and self-organization. Salomon also relied on small project teams, some of just three or four people, as a means to stimulate initiative and responsibility.

Most European innovators rely on small teams to develop innovation. Michelin has managed its two most important innovative projects in recent years through small teams led by creative people, to whom are given time, resources and independence from established core R&D units. Similarly, the successes of Salomon are the result of small teams protected by management and somewhat removed from day-to-day business pressures. This does not mean that they did not work under pressure, but rather that the pressure was related more to the need to transform a vision into what Georges Salomon refers to as a 'cult product' than the short-term pressures of the market.

Trumpf is another firm which emphasizes team work; one of the firm's guiding principles for organizational projects is that 'teamwork and close co-operation between team members, and between teams and those employees working in other organizational units, have a greater pay-off than individualistic, competition-based behaviour. One of the more unusual examples is Mondragón, which is made up of three divisions, several clusters and a number of small co-operatives. While the market is usually attacked by clusters with critical mass, innovation typically happens in the smaller units, the co-operatives. There might be all kind of horizontal linkages and top-down stimulus, but the real innovative work is done, in most instances, by small teams down in the focused co-operatives.

Of course team approaches are also common in American and Japanese companies. The team approach is a key aspect of corporate culture at Microsoft, where as one manager commented: 'Our culture has been: I'm going to get a small band of guys together and against all odds I'm going to build this great product'. As Microsoft products have grown in sophistication and have increasingly had to be compatible, product development requires the simultaneous efforts of multiple teams. Excellence in overall systems, not excellence in individual design, is the most important qualitative aspect of innovation, necessitating very close co-operation not only between members of an individual team but also between teams.

Team work is also very important in Japanese companies, but with a slightly different emphasis. In Japanese companies, knowledge creation tends to start with individual efforts. Highly subjective insights, intuitions and hunches are at the root of knowledge creation and innovation. To nurture rich insights and intuitions, a knowledge-creating company requires diversity in the pool of talents available within the company. This diversity enhances requisite variety, which is one of the enabling conditions for the organization. The result is the creation of a 'knowledge crew', a team which partakes of this requisite variety and can bring a variety of skills and a density of knowledge to a project. The crew members who worked on Nissan's Primera project had this variety; one of the engineers had studied at Berlin Technical College and was fluent in both German and English, another member had studied at the University of Glasgow and was married to a British national and yet another member, an exterior designer, had studied at London's Royal College of Arts. These educational backgrounds as well as individuals' familiarity with Europe proved to be an asset in working with Europeans on the Primera project.

All this having been said, there are subtle but real differences in how these flat organizations and teams are employed in the innovation process. In particular, there are differences in how teams and the organization are controlled. Flat structures may be becoming universal and teams may be becoming the most relied upon business unit, but in European companies, at least, top down control and direction remains strong. Individuals and teams are encouraged towards self-expression, creativity and innovation, but they do so within a hierarchy created by planning and by the leader's vision.

Nowhere is this more obvious than at Psion, an entrepreneurial company which does not have a strongly hierarchical management. What it does have is what might be termed a 'hierarchy of innovation' cascading down through various levels from vision to materialization. In Psion, everything happens at the top. The technological vision, and the market context for that vision, is inevitably provided by the founder and CEO, David Potter. From Potter come the creative ideas; from the development teams come the materialization of those ideas. Potter's role is to embed his vision in the minds of the development team and then to motivate them to take that vision forward. Ideas are typically brainstormed by a nucleus of engineers who all have a product perspective, who then work towards materializing products. Other top managers at Psion are intimately involved in the development process. As Psion's quality manager explains:

> We are slightly unusual in the way that we operate. David Potter has the creative ideas. My role is that of head of engineering, but I'm in fact the catalyst for diverse activities. I see myself as a generalist. While Charles Davies [research and development director] is in overall charge of development, he is also responsible for software development. Collie Myers is technical director, responsible for the electronics, and I'm responsible for product and system design. As our people see it, Charles is the 'head', the

thinker, Collie is the heart – he feels whether things are right – and I'm the 'hands', the doer.

There is a difference too in the use of team work in Europe compared to Japan and America. In Europe, creative teams are often isolated from day-to-day activity. Their close association with top management gives them protection and a special immunity; if properly resourced, these teams can become true innovation centres in their own right. Referring to the C3M process, a real breakthrough in manufacturing and cost cutting, François Michelin describes how he gave his engineering team the 'freedom to make it happen' by separating them from the rest of the company and letting them work alone. European teams also tend to be homogeneous in content and closely tied to their own company culture: they are, in a real sense, an elite.

At Microsoft, as mentioned above, responsibility for innovation is pushed down to teams working at a lower level. These teams, while also homogeneous in content, tend to be less protected from day-to-day marketing and competitive pressures and are much more part of the 'mainstream' of the company. In Japan, teams are deliberately formed incorporating a great deal of variety. The company's culture is often virtually the only homogeneous element. However, Kao and Sharp do place some of their innovative workers in isolation from the rest of the company. Sharp organizes its R&D activities on three levels, the Corporate R&D Group, Business Group labs and Business Division labs, separated on the basis of the time frame required for technological and/or product development; Corporate R&D Group takes on longer term projects, while Business Division labs work on projects of one and one-half years or less. Sharp also uses project teams outside the conventional business hierarchy and transfers information and knowledge back and forth between the two.

The picture that emerges, then, is one of distinctive difference in the use of team work in Europe compared to Japan and America. In Europe, creative teams are isolated from day to day activity and protected by top management that gives them a special immunity. European teams seem to be homogeneous in content and closely tied to the company's culture; in this sense they could be considered to be elites within companies, placed in close contact (often including close physical proximity) with the top managers who in turn provide the drive and impetus for innovation.

Resources: The Allocation of Resources to Support Innovation

Top management does more than just have vision; it also plays a critical role in turning that vision into reality by allocating extensive resources toward R&D. In firm after firm in the study, it was noted that very high levels of resources had been devoted to R&D in terms of both funds and key staff. At Mondragón, the importance of resource allocation to R&D was reflected in firm's research centre at Ikelan, created specifically to strengthen corporate innovation. At IBM, Kao, Michelin and many others, the stated importance of innovation was supported by the allocation of extensive resources.

In many firms, R&D spending exceeded the average for firms in the industry and was often well above that of close competitors. Salomon spends 7% of turnover on R&D, compared with 3.5% for its closest rival, Rossignol; Michelin spends 4%, compared to 2.8% for Bridgestone; Trumpf spends 8% compared with the 1–2% on average for the machine tool industry in the USA, Europe and Japan. Mondragón's leading clusters spend 3–5% while their surrounding competitors average 1–2%. One notable factor in the study was that firms where top managers are also leading shareholders or key decision makers spend more on R&D than their competitors, and the priority assigned to innovation within the firm is strongly reinforced.

Incentivization: A Reward Structure that Supports Innovative Behaviour

Coupled with an emphasis on the long-term approach and stability, many innovative firms also offer rewards and incentives for innovative behaviour. Microsoft's strong reliance on stock grants to offset salaries that are somewhat below the industry mean reflects its policy of linking pay with corporate performance. Other firms in the United States use similar measures; at Johnson & Johnson, for example, organizational subdivision results in small units where managers are compensated based on the performance of their unit.

Some European firms also make use of systems of incentive and reward. At Bertelsmann, for example, an elaborate system ties rewards to individual responsibility, with an average of 50% of compensation on variable elements and with rewards based on individual or group performance. At other firms, both European and Japanese, the use of formal incentive and reward systems was less strongly in evidence, suggesting that this policy is less widespread than others outlined above. The use of pay-for-performance mechanisms remains better accepted in the United States than elsewhere, where performance is not so directly tied to pay. Yet not all rewards need be financial: the key principle is to identify and reward desired behaviour, so that employees feel that desired behaviour is linked with certain outcomes.

Virtually all the European innovators studied had a human resources management approach which aimed to boost innovation. People were selected, hired, trained, evaluated, promoted and rewarded for innovation. Michelin looks for people who want a life-long career, and the company seeks to fit the job with the person rather than the opposite; rotation and training of personnel through special assignments, cross-functionally and internationally, are part of the acculturation process, and individual potential receives detailed attention. Nurturing innovative talent, like the nurturing of innovation itself, is a key concern of top management. François Michelin's conviction is that new ideas are fragile and frequently in opposition to current belief; thus the company identifies creative individuals and offers them step-by-step enlarged responsibilities following project developments.

At Trumpf, two criteria play an important role in personnel selection: employees should have an excellent education, and Trumpf sets a high value on the traits and value orientation of the candidates. Employees and managers should have internalized already the values which form the basis of Trumpf's corporate culture, for example unpretentiousness, a sense of duty, openness, performance-orientation, self-confidence and unselfishness. Generally, Trumpf pursues a policy of promotion from within, and the company runs its own training centre. In terms of rewards, Trumpf management believes that the introduction of variable compensation elements for proposals and single achievements would be dysfunctional, because it would endanger elements of the corporate culture; it is assumed that professionals do not usually put as much value on monetary rewards as on the chance to do challenging work, to achieve and to be creative.

Bertelsmann also puts a high value on individual profiles and skills. Candidates for managerial positions should have academic training at high level, such as a doctorate in business administration. Bertelsmann also looks for entrepreneurial potential; future managers should have strong analytical skills, the ability to convince others and, above all, creativity. On average, only three or four candidates out of 1200 are employed. Junior managers get the opportunity to develop their potential on the job, and Bertelsmann pursues the policy of promotion from within. Unlike Trumpf, however, Bertelsmann emphasizes the importance of an entrepreneurial incentive system which was designed as a fine-tuned model of rewards and punishments. Managing directors receive a good deal of their compensation in variable form linked to short and long-term performance criteria. Bad performance can result in punishment through reduction of fixed income levels.

Equifinality: Different Roads to a Common Destination

The revealing of common success factors among innovative firms around the world can only be welcomed. What this means is that no firm is necessarily handicapped by its geography or national origin; rather, most firms, by taking a careful and persistent approach that combines top management commitment, resource allocation, organizational structure and supporting mechanisms, can improve their records as innovators. There is no 'one best way' to innovation, and there is no one best organization for innovation; innovative firms have been found equally among Spanish co-operatives, Italian family-owned firms, French industrial giants and British start-ups.

The innovative firms in this study have retained and built upon their local identities to achieve their present profile. Esaote has drawn on Italian state supported research and local network relationships to achieve a profile of a modern innovative company. Banco Santander has made use of Spanish values of pride and paternalism as it evolved into a modern innovative company. Psion drew upon the paradox of British eccentricity and British conservatism as a way to achieve the delicate balances of individual and group, stability and pressure, that describe the high-performing innovative firm. These and other firms neither repressed nor ignored what was distinctive in their local environment, but made use of local qualities in order to achieve a broader set of common features. These firms gave expression to local traits while pursuing a similar objective. Thus, instead of equality, we might better think in terms of equifinality; that is, taking different roads to a common end.

Despite the importance of similarities among the firms studied, and despite the conclusion that they have many features in common, it would be too simple to suggest that local features are not important. Although the firms studied share a number of common features, they have not renounced their local identities. They have not somehow become 'world' companies without local bonds. Just because they have several common features, Michelin is not any less of a French company, Trumpf is no less German and Kao is no less Japanese. Returning to the metaphors with which we began this chapter, a Gothic cathedral and a Buddhist temple fulfil many of the same functions, but that does not mean they are similar; paintings by Michelangelo and Magritte make similar use of perspective, light and shade but tell very different stories.

Part 2

Diversity

Chapter 9

Shadows of the Pyrenees:
Describing Diversity

*Things which are truths on one side of the Pyrenees may be
falsehoods on the other.*

Blaise Pascal

Introduction

Culture casts a long shadow. Its consequences affect every
aspect of our lives, including, as Geert Hofstede (1980,
1991) has so persuasively described, the ways in which we
organize and do business. In the last two decades, it has become
fashionable to argue that cultures around the world are
beginning to converge; improvements in global communications are bridging cultural gaps and the information revolution
is bringing us closer together. The counter-argument, however,
is that although on many levels the world is becoming smaller,
improved and increased contact between cultures is merely
serving to highlight cultural differences; the more we are drawn
together by globalization, the more we are aware of cultural
variety between and within nations. The more we know about
each other, the more we realize how different we are.

Cultural variety and diversity are now accepted as a major
issue in international business, and the last few years have seen

113

an explosion of works on this subject. In the mid-1980s, Kenichi Ohmae published what has now become a classic delineation of major economic powers. Ohmae's 'triad' included three pillars of the global economy, Japan, the USA and Europe, each with its own distinctive characteristics. More recently attention has been paid to other business cultures outside the Triad; China and the overseas Chinese community, for example, have attracted attention from writers such as Whitley (1992), Redding (1990), Ng, Tung, Chen (1995) Child (1994) and Bond (1986, 1991). Finally, writers such as Hofstede, Porter (1990), Hampden-Turner and Trompenaars (1995), Whitley (1992), Kogut (1993) Cavaleri and Obłój (1993) and Hickson and Pugh (1993) have looked at cultural differences on a global basis, and at their consequences for management. Although it is still often seen as a barrier rather than a source of competitive advantage, global and regional diversity is nevertheless accepted as a fact of modern business life.

This acceptance is not before time. The imperative for innovation was described in Chapter 2; the imperative for companies and organizations to come to terms with diversity and make it work for them is equally powerful. Innovation ultimately depends on how companies acquire and use knowledge, and on the nature of that knowledge itself, two areas in which cultural forces have a particularly powerful impact. How we learn is influenced by the social conditions under which learning takes place, while how we use our learning is influenced by the organizations and structures within which we work. Any understanding of innovation in the world today must begin by understanding and accepting diversity, realizing that there is no one best way to innovation and seeking paths which are most right for the firm, its managers and its culture.

Similarity and Diversity

However, recognizing and analysing diversity does not mean that we need attempt to deny or downplay the importance of global similarities. The existence of similarities is both factual and important; one of the most intriguing results of the thirteen case studies was the fact that many of the apparent differences in organization and practice between firms turned out on closer inspection to be similarities. Companies of vastly different origin or size turn out to not only have very similar attitudes to innovation but also use very similar organizational structures and strategies to achieve innovation and creativity.

Similarity and diversity are powerful forces, and both have a role to play. Unfortunately this idea is not always recognized, and many recent arguments in management have focused on either similarity or diversity as extremes. In advertising, for example, two polarized positions have appeared: one camp argues that global markets exist and that multinationals are justified in using standardized generic advertising in every market, while the opposite party argue that regional and national diversity mean standardization is impossible and that companies ought logically to customize their advertising for each individual local market. In fact, as Harris (1995) has shown, most companies adopt a pragmatic mix of strategies, using some generic advertising elements in most markets and then tailoring the advertisements for specific markets.

One way of understanding the relationship between similarity and different levels of diversity is to look at language. All the major languages of Europe and the Middle East (and by extension the dominant languages of America) are descended from one root language, Indo-European. Within the Indo-European descent, however, there are a number of different linguistic families, such as the Romance languages, descended from Latin, and the Germanic languages. Each of these families is in turn broken down into individual languages, such as French, Spanish and Italian (Romance) and German, Dutch and English (Germanic). At a still lower level, languages have different accents and dialects, some of which are almost mutually incomprehensible and many of which are influenced by other languages (examples include Gaelic influences on the English spoken in Scotland or Greek influences on the Italian dialect of Calabria). At the same time, all these languages have many common elements; many of the root words are the same, and different languages have borrowed and adopted words from each other at all three levels.

The same effect can be seen in business. Some similarities spring from the fact that all businesses are run by human beings and, at some fundamental level, all human beings do things in basically the same way; at the same time, diversity develops on a variety of levels due to environmental, cultural and personal differences.

At a global level, our study found many common features among innovative firms. The firms studied, be they European, Japanese or American, were similar in their strategic approaches to innovation. Each had a strong leader with a clear vision of what innovation meant to the company; each backed this vision with long-term resource commitments; all adopted organization structures designed to facilitate innovation, in particular through enhanced information sharing mechanisms, and all had adopted reward structures which supported innovative behaviour.

These similarities, which we term *global success factors*, have been explored in detail in the previous chapter. Their presence should come as no surprise. The fundamentally similar approaches to innovation adopted by the companies in the sample are simply a reflection of the deeper similarities which characterize virtually all international businesses. Despite variances in geography, history, culture and organization, most businesses are fundamentally similar in appearance and share many common goals.

The Two Fallacies

The strength of these similarities is considerable, so much so that many observers have been tempted to concentrate on them and ignore differences. If we focus on similarities only, we can postulate that all businesses not only look similar but *are* similar. From there it is a short step to a model of an ideal business, and then of an ideal form of management. Diversity then becomes nothing more than a challenge to overcome, a series of obstacles to be ironed out. One of the fallacies of this approach, however, is the *fallacy of halves*: similarities are only half the picture. All fingerprints look superficially similar but each one is unique; every business has similarities with other businesses and unique characteristics all its own.

The other fallacy is what might be termed the *realist fallacy*, which assumes that the similarities we see in global business are reflections of an ideal type of business, that somewhere the perfect business model exists and all we have to do is work towards it. In fact, the similarities which are so apparent today are reflections instead of a historical heritage. The modern business, in the form that it exists around the world, is essentially the result of the tradition of European innovation alluded to in the prologue.

Levels of Geographical Diversity

Our initial way of exploring diversity is through geographical divisions. Starting at the global level, where we have looked for similarities and common truths rather than differences, we can narrow our focus down through regional, national and intra-national or local levels. As the focus narrows, diversity becomes more pronounced. Each of these levels fits into the next level, like Russian dolls: provinces or states nest within nations, nations within regions and regions within the world as a whole.

At the global level, innovative firms in all parts of the world may share certain characteristics. Such features can be thought of as universal in their applicability and include factors such as strong leadership and long-term strategies for innovation.

Diversity first appears at the regional level. Firms in the three major industrial regions – Europe, Japan and North America – differ in important ways. Strong leadership, for example, may have different definitions and different leadership attributes may be regarded as important in each region.

Going down within Europe to the national level, we find significant differences among innovative firms in various European nations. Some of these differences may be specific to a single nation (features may be found only in Germany but in no other European country, or only in Italy and nowhere else), or they may be found in some European regions but not others (such as in Italy, France and Spain, but not in the UK or Germany).

Fourth, important differences may exist at the intra-national level, that is, among firms located in different parts of the same country, such as provinces, counties or states. For instance, to speak of the United Kingdom may be a useful abstraction in some ways, yet important differences exist between England and Scotland, and even between the north and south of England. Mondragón's unique characteristics are not so much Spanish as Basque; Esaote acknowledges the difference in style between its Genoese base and the 'Umbrian' model of its Florentine operations. In Belgium there are important differences between the French-speaking and Flemish-speaking regions; in Germany there are differences between the north and Bavaria, in Spain between Catalonia and Asturias, in Italy between Sicily and Tuscany. The list does not end there; similar differences can be found within every other European nation, and making generalizations about differences among nations is complicated indeed.

Common Ground, Diverse Culture

The geographical analysis of diversity is a useful tool for highlighting different aspects of diversity. It should be noted, however, that some cultural traits do not fit tidily within these concentric levels. For instance, Anglo-Saxon culture and language, which may be an important cultural basis for economic behaviour, are shared to at least some extent by the

UK (a European nation), the United States and Canada (North America), and Australia and New Zealand (Oceania). Similarly, religions such as Islam, Judaism, or Catholicism may be important bases of economic behaviour and may cut across regional or national lines. Looking for evidence of innovative behaviour that is associated with geography is thus a difficult task, as we are faced with many different ways to aggregate or divide by geography; it is necessary also to look at other factors such as social, psychological and economic differences.

National boundaries are important, if only because they mark the extent of governmental authority, and in Europe at least, governments often play a strong role in supporting the innovation process: witness Esaote's emergence from a state sector background. An easy metaphor for describing different types of diversity and the importance of boundaries can be found in Weber, who developed a fourfold classification of rationalism. Applying this same classification to diversity, we see the following:

- *Formalized* diversity: the physical borders between nations.
- *Substantive* diversity: this exists in the form of different religions and social attitudes; the divide between Protestant north and Catholic south is a classic example, but north–south and east–west divides exist within individual nations as well.
- *Practical* diversity: this is imposed by considerations such as language or geography; the Pyrenees or the English Channel constitute practical barriers between parts of Europe.
- *Theoretical* diversity: this results when people in different parts of Europe place emphasis on different abstract concepts. Thus education systems in Germany place a strong emphasis on science and engineering and these are considered prestigious disciplines, whereas in Britain more university students are attracted to the humanities.

However, it is important to remember that these boundaries are permeable. Economic and political integration is reducing the

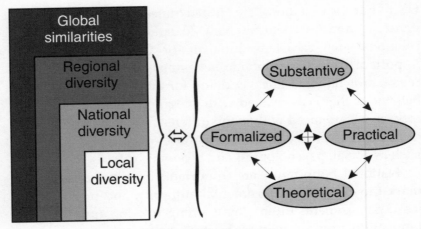

Figure 9.1 Diversity

impact of national borders, while greater travel and exposure to other lifestyles and ways of thought are reducing the impact of the other three forms. Europeans of substantial income have always been multicultural and have moved easily (in times of peace, at least) between countries and cultures; in the late twentieth century, this facility is becoming acquired by the bulk of the population. The future of European diversity is likely to see more dynamism, more breaking down of barriers and more management across frontiers. It remains to be seen what the cost in terms of loss of social uniqueness will be.

The question is, will globalization lead to homogenization, to an ironing out of the differences between cultures? It seems unlikely. The decline in importance of national borders is blurring the distinction between nations, but it seems unlikely in the short run, at least, to eradicate the differences between cultures. Relative differences may change; but for the time being, it seems likely that the main consequence of innovation will simply be to make Europeans more aware of and better able to manage diversity itself. Indeed, the more exposure European innovators and firms have to practices in the rest of the world, the more diverse influences they will be able to harness and – in theory at least – the more competitive they will become.

Chapter 10

The Reef, the Garden and the Forest: The Diversity of the Triad

At a regional level, we find that perceptions of the enterprise begin to vary with the nature of the society in which the enterprise functions. Hampden-Turner and Trompenaars (1993) comment that in the United States, an enterprise is conceived of primarily as 'a system designed to perform functions and tasks in an efficient way, while in Japan it is thought as a group of people working together'. In other words, in the American context the organization is mainly seen as an 'economic machine' while in Japan it is a 'social organism'. American orthodoxy assumes the organization to be 'an island in the sea of the market', surrounded by competitors who are determined to take away the firm's customers or even prey shark-like on the firm itself. The American context can be compared to a coral reef: a business environment of great size and complexity which has evolved almost naturally and without restriction, full of niches where small firms can embed themselves yet full also of dangerous predators. In Japan, on the other hand, the firm is embedded in a web of various institutions; here we could choose as our metaphor a Zen garden, where various elements exist together in harmony with each other and their environment.

The European context is more complex, quite simply because it is more heterogeneous than that of either America or Japan. Nevertheless, we can make some generalizations. The impact of history, particularly the historical evolution of the modern business model alluded to in the prologue, has been very strong, even stronger in than in Japan which, despite its ancient culture, has in business terms made a break with its past.

A metaphor for Europe, then, might be that of an ancient forest, full of great trees in whose shadow many different species thrive, old and established yet constantly changing. Older, more complex, more diverse and more structured than either America or Japan, the European business scene is so rich and dense as to almost defy categorization. We shall look first at the two more homogeneous regions, America and Japan, before moving on to Europe.

The American Context

The United States, shares a common Judaeo-Christian heritage with Europe and, at least until recently, drew most of its immigrants and its dominant cultural heritage from Europe (Reich, 1983), yet it is distinct from its parent region in a number of key ways. In contrast with the emphasis on the past in Europe, there is in America an equally strong orientation towards the future. There is a faith, sometimes implicit but often clearly stated, that the future will be – and indeed should be – better than the present. Perfectibilism, the doctrine that human society is in a state of constant progress towards an ultimate good, the primary exponent of which was the French philosopher the Marquis de Condorcet, was introduced into the nascent American state in the eighteenth century. Within twenty years of American independence, Condorcet was dead, executed during the Terror in France, and a few years later, Thomas Malthus's *Essay on the General Principles of Population* exploded the perfectibilist myth in Europe; but in America the idea has survived, at least in modified form.

There remains in America a sense of the frontier, a pioneer spirit of adventure and boundless progress. The millions who flocked to America in the eighteenth century believed in a promised land, free of the wars, poverty and persecution which they endured in their homelands. Somewhere along the way the concept of a land of opportunity and future promise became embedded in the American psyche; one need only listen to recordings of any US presidential campaign speech over the past century to catch echoes of this. At the same time, related to future orientation is an orientation toward achievement. In contrast with a tradition of social stratification and elites, there is in America an emphasis on individual achievement. This achievement orientation is related to a basic importance placed on pragmatism, which again is a counter-point to the European tradition of intellectualism and abstract thought; Americans tend to be impatient with ideology and theory for theory's sake, and place an emphasis on practical, working results.

In fact, this pragmatism has been one of America's great strengths, and has in no small measure been responsible for the rise of the United States to the position of premier world power. Part of the enduring image of the United States is of a nation full of ingenious entrepreneurs. 'Yankee ingenuity', 'know-how', the 'can-do spirit'; these are clichés which have been associated with American businessmen and traders since at least the mid-eighteenth century. A fascination with machinery and technology has led to the building of enduring folk myths around characters such as Benjamin Franklin, Samuel Colt, Thomas Edison and the Wright brothers. Technology became a kind of alternative frontier, a frontier which could be explored through the mind alone as opposed to the physical frontier of the American West.

Paradoxically, during the great years of American industrial growth its innovations were largely borrowed ones. In the words of Reich (1983: 47):

In the half century spanning 1870 and 1920, a major invention made its appearance in America, on average, once every fifteen months. Most of these inventions were based on British discoveries; American inventors merely applied these discoveries to specific products and processes.

The best-known example is probably the development of the automobile industry. Europeans invented the first working motor cars, and were indeed the first to begin making and selling them commercially. However, car manufacturing was transformed by Americans such as Henry Ford, using the new techniques of scientific management, and making the US car industry dominant in the world for decades. Reich contrasts American scientific management which aimed at simplified production with its European counterpart, exemplified by Fayol, the goal of which was effective supervision.

Two other aspects of American business culture deserve comment in the context of innovation. One is self-reliance and independence which, when allied to technical accomplishment, leads to the kind of 'can-do' culture which is so effective at exploiting innovation. It can also lead to an intolerance of bureaucracy and hierarchy, and a distrust of government. The second aspect is the strong egalitarian tradition. Equality and democracy are, of course, fundamental to the American political system and explicit in its constitution, which guarantees free speech to all and equality of representation in government. This same egalitarian tradition is also manifested in the economic system, which has been described by d'Iribarne (1989) as based on 'free exchange among equals'. Just as a system of free expression is an open marketplace of ideas, the economic system is a marketplace of free exchange among equal parties. Related to economic freedom in turn is a strong sense of individual rewards for individual achievement. The use of incentive pay and performance bonuses have become widespread in the United States, not surprising in a society where individual rewards for individual contribution seem appropriate.

Innovation and entrepreneurship continue to go hand in hand. Colt with his patented revolvers, Edison with the electric light and phonograph did more than just invent new things; they found ways of exploiting these innovations, converting individual ideas into mass market production. Many say this is the great American strength. None typifies it more today than Bill Gates, the CEO of Microsoft, who began as a computer programmer at the age of 14, wrote the BASIC language with a former classmate and now controls a multi-billion dollar software corporation which sets, for the moment, at least, the standard for operating systems worldwide.

The Japanese Context

Unlike the United States, Japan has distinct social and historical antecedents. Japanese society is characterized by its relative homogeneity and by its emphasis on the group rather than the individual, perhaps rooted in the imperatives of rice cultivation, a group exercise where members are highly dependent on each other. In contradistinction to the European tendency toward intellectualism and American pragmatism, the Japanese approach may be described as incremental experimentation, or learning by doing. In Japanese innovation, we see the successful alliance of an ancient culture with modern technology.

Although it is a homogeneous culture, Japan has its share of borrowings, and nowhere is this more apparent than in the world of business. Though Japan's culture is complex and sophisticated, it was for centuries virtually frozen. In the late sixteenth century, following the first contact with the West through Portuguese missionaries and traders, the *shoguns* virtually sealed Japan from foreign contact, and for another three hundred years Japan was a society where time meant little. Social systems and organizations showed little or no evolution, and most Japanese had no knowledge of the world beyond their own islands.

All this began to change when, in 1853, the 'black ships' of the US Navy under Commodore Perry arrived in Tokyo Bay and forced the first, limited opening of Japan to foreign influence. It took another twenty-five years for change to really began, but when it did begin it happened with unprecedented speed. The catalyst for change was the Emperor Meiji, who broke the power of the *shoguns* and ruled Japan directly. There have been few more important innovators in the history of any nation, or indeed the world.

The emperor and his advisors looked at the technological achievements of the West and realized the gulf that lay between them and Japan. Japan's only chance of retaining its importance, and indeed its independence in the age of colonialism, was to catch up to the West as soon as possible. To achieve this, the emperor introduced not only Western technology but Western social mechanisms and forms of organization as well. Not all of these were suited to Japanese culture and society and not all were successful, but one import from the West was supremely successful: the corporation.

The new Japanese industrialists became adroit at introducing American and European business techniques, trying them and then adapting them to their own needs. A prime example can be found in Tokuji Hayakawa, who set up a metalworks in Tokyo in 1912 and invented the Ever-Sharp pencil in 1915; today the company he founded is called Sharp, not in honour of the founder but in honour of his first innovation. After 1945, with much of Japanese industry in ruins and the American occupation forces initially controlling every aspect of government and economy, the level of scanning and borrowing from foreign environments became even more pronounced. In some cases Japanese firms began borrowing foreign techniques even before they had been adopted in their home countries; the case of Deming is probably the most famous example, but others can be found as well. All this fits well into the concept of incremental experimentation; Japanese firms constantly 'tinker' with their systems, trying out new methods, rather than seeking for great leaps forward.

The establishment and progressive adaptation of Western business and Western technology revolutionized Japan as it was intended to do, and the alliance of state and corporation has since served as a precedent for rapid development in many other countries of east Asia. In the late nineteenth century, and even more in the decades of rebuilding following the Second World War, the corporation became not only a source of national wealth but a critically important social organization. Japanese paternalism fitted well with the hierarchical structure of corporations, while simultaneously the communal nature of Japanese society helped develop an organic system whereby workers and managers from many different backgrounds pooled their knowledge and worked for the greater good of the organization. The group, in Japanese business, has always been far more important than the individual, and it was this group dynamic which has lain behind Japanese successes in industries such as automobiles and electronics.

To see the difference between this entrepreneurial culture and that of the United States, one need only look at the difference in their origins. In the United States, a country founded on independence and self-reliance, entrepreneurship became seen as the ultimate form of self-actualization. In Japan, business is a communal activity aimed at achieving a common good. The goal of the Kao Corporation, founded in 1890 as a maker of soap and still concentrating on soaps, detergents, cosmetics and personal hygiene products, is 'cleanliness, health and beauty'. The management philosophy of Microsoft exhibits a strong future orientation, a high emphasis on pragmatism and very high incentives for performance, all of which are entirely consistent with American society and reflective of its values. By contrast, the philosophy espoused by Kao, with its explicit principles of service to the customer, absolute egalitarianism and search for truth and the integration of individual's wisdom, seem quite natural for a Japanese firm; yet they would seem odd in an American firm.

In both of these examples, firm characteristics would seem to typify the distinctive qualities of their region. The United

States, although a genetically diverse country (a 'melting pot'), has been culturally inspired by a unique dream which has tended to create homogeneity. Perhaps because America is a nation of immigrants, whose citizens (with the notable exceptions of African-Americans) chose to come to America's shores for a better life, Americans tend to have a strong future orientation. There is a faith, sometimes implicit but often clearly stated, that the future will be – and indeed should be – better than the present. Japan is even more homogeneous, largely because it is a single country with common historical roots. The Japanese perspective is grounded largely on Confucian dynamism, with its values of persistence, status, thrift and avoidance of shame.

The European Context

> Looking through most American and Japanese eyes, there is no such thing as Europeans *per se*; they see only the *diversity* of Europe. That is because they are looking out from relatively homogeneous societies. In contrast, European society is an incredible jumble of cultures, languages and traditions. But when Europeans step back from their national borders and look *through their own eyes* at how and where they fit into the world, the similarities that bind Europeans together become very clear. As a top executive at Lyonnaise des Eaux-Dumez remarked, 'There are enormous differences between a Dane and a Greek, but you only need one trip to the United States to realize they are both Europeans.' (Bloom, Calori and de Woot, 1994: 17)

Studies of European business culture almost immediately run up against the problem of heterogeneity. However, it is possible to isolate certain characteristics which are notably European. Calori and de Woot (1994) list six common features:

- Orientation towards people

- Internal negotiation
- Managing international diversity
- Managing between extremes
- Strong product orientation
- Less formal systems of management

Orientation towards People

Calori and de Woot's study found that European firms place a strong emphasis on the importance of the individual. Employees and managers tend to have more personal freedom than in Japanese or even American firms, and there is a greater tolerance of personal idiosyncrasies and non-conformism. Coupled with this is a strong sense of responsibility on the part of firms towards their employees; at the macro level this can be seen in the social market economic models prevalent in many European countries. The result can be a strong bonding between firms and employees, where the latter both have greater security and the freedom to create and be innovative.

Internal Negotiation

Another result, however, is the emergence of strong stakeholder groups within firms. The strong individuals within firms are also usually well-educated, and their minds have been trained in a system which encourages debate, questioning and discussion. European managers need to be able to negotiate with and convince their employees in order to obtain their involvement. Diplomacy and the ability to explain ideas clearly are both required, and there is a correspondingly greater emphasis on personal leadership style over management skills.

Managing International Diversity

One of the consequences of heterogeneity is to give many European businessmen the experience of coping with diversity: indeed, many European managers have to do this earlier than do their American or Japanese counterparts (though this relative experience must be tempered by the fact that many American companies, including those that are solely domestic in scope, have a multicultural workforce). With many nations and many cultures in a relatively small geographical area, and with most of those nations being quite small in terms of population and markets, European firms tend to go work across national borders at an earlier stage in their development. European managers are used to diversity; many of them even like it. They are less likely to see international diversity as an obstacle, and more likely to view it as a source of strength or advantage.

Managing between Extremes

In the eyes of European managers, at least, American and Japanese business cultures can be considered as opposites: individual versus team-based, short-term outlook versus long-term outlook, entrepreneurial versus communal. They see themselves as being between these two extremes, partaking of something of both positions. For example, team-based approaches and individualism are not seen as opposites, but rather as mutually compatible. Similarly, an outlook which is more long-term than that of the Americans but less so than that of the Japanese leads to quite different approaches to the cycle of creation, orientation and elaboration.

Strong Product Orientation

Although there are many exceptions, particularly in Britain, European companies tend to be strongly focused on products and product design. Many top managers tend to be from scientific or engineering backgrounds; in keeping with the European tradition, they often have a passion for science and technology and are keen to translate that passion into inventions and products. The pursuit of truth, goodness and beauty infuses their actions. On the other hand, this pursuit can sometimes lead to a neglect of customer focus; European firms are less likely to be marketing-driven than their American counterparts, in particular.

Less Formal Systems of Management

In Europe – and again there are exceptions – management tends to be less formal and more intuitive. As noted above, there is more of an emphasis on leadership style and less on formal skills; similarly, management systems tend to be less structured than in American firms and particularly Japanese firms. It is probable that this is a reflection of the historical evolvement of European business models, which emphasized either family control, which requires less formality, or tight personal control by a single owner-manager (Calori and de Woot, 1994).

This last point is a particularly interesting one. Logically, the United States with its culture of independence and freedom should be less formal in its management systems while Europe, with its strong social hierarchies and class systems, should be more so. In fact, the opposite is the case. Ritzer (1993) argues that it is in America that the formal-rational bureaucracies described by Weber have developed to their fullest extent (particularly, he says, in the fast food restaurant industry) and blames this development on Taylorism and scientific management which introduced a strong formal-rationalist element into business. Recent American management writers such as Tom Peters and Rosabeth Moss Kanter have argued that American companies need to break down their own hierarchies if they are to become more competitive. Europe, it would seem, might have a slight advantage in terms of requisite structure.

Europe can also be described as primarily ascriptive culture rather than a primarily achievement culture. This does not mean that in European countries the ascribing of status to priority over achievement is necessarily a negation of achievement itself; rather, it means that the past is highly valuable to Europeans. This explains why they are inclined to reconcile achievement 'to ascribe ways that make in achieving more likely than it might otherwise be' (Hampden-Turner and

	America	Japan	Europe
LEADERSHIP	Leader/elected leader as controller	Leader as servant	Leader as owner/father
HIERARCHY	Individual	Team	Bureaucracy
INNOVATION	All company	All company	Elites

Figure 10.1 Regional characteristics

Trompenaars, 1993). The Mondragón cooperative shows a good example of this. The Mondragón experience developed between 1943 and 1956 under the leadership of a priest, José-Maria Arizmendiarreta. Mondragón, a town in a valley in the heart of the Basque Country, had a high rate of unemployment in the early 1940s. In the area, however, there was an important industrial culture. The Mondragón dynamic can be seen as coming from an alliance between the Catholic Church and industrial technology, between an ascriptive and an achievement culture.

Leadership from the Centre

As discussed in Chapter 8, leadership plays a critical role in the innovation process. However, different cultures have very different ideas as to what leadership is. In Japan, the leader has traditionally been seen (at least in Buddhist philosophy) as a servant, whose responsibilities are to those beneath him or her, and in some cases to those further up the hierarchy; historically, all owed service to the emperor. American tradition is quite different; in most field of activity leaders owe their position in America to democratic mandate, and retain that mandate only so long as they are able to satisfy the electorate. Scientific management to some extent replaced this paradigm in business with one of scientific, hierarchical control in which the leader sits at the top of a chain of command and in which responsibility to the lower levels has been curtailed or even abolished. American firms tend to follow one of these two models.

The European model is rooted in historical traditions of feudal and military service where the leader typically led from the front. The person of the leader, not the institution, is the prime focus. From the late eighteenth century this tradition was modified by the countervailing revolutionary tradition, and leaders began to work more closely with their subordinates to achieve harmony. European leaders owe a duty to their subordinates more for societal reasons rather than for political or philosophical reasons. The strongly personal style, however, remains.

At Psion and Versace, the leader is the prime innovator, directly responsible for much of the firm's creative success. Georges Salomon has in the past been personally responsible for developing successful products and retains a close interest; Berthold Leibinger and François Michelin are technically accomplished, and one of Castellano's top team leaders at Esaote, Fabrizio Landi, is a scientist and engineer. Even where there is no direct connection, as at Bertelsmann, the concept of leadership from the centre remains a key guiding philosophy; innovators are free to innovate, so long as they do so within the structures laid down from above. Again in contrast, the leaders of Kao and Sharp do not directly concern themselves with innovation and Bill Gates, a talented innovator in his own right, now spends at least half of his time negotiating with and managing his project teams rather than directly involving himself in innovation projects.

Family Ownership

A recent survey of French companies shows that two-thirds of the largest firms in France are partly or wholly-owned by families, and in about one-quarter of all cases a family member or members directly manages the firm. In the nine European firms above, the founder or a close relative or descendant controlled the firm in six cases (Psion, Salomon, Michelin, Versace, Esaote, Banco de Santander), although it should be added in the case of Psion and Esaote that other members of the founder's family were not closely involved; instead, a tight-knit professional top team played a similar role. Of the three exceptions, Bertelsmann is still largely controlled by the founding family, although they play little direct role in daily operations; Trumpf's chief executive also owns a majority stake, and one of his senior directors is also his son-in-law; and Mondragón is still managed by close personal friends and associates of the founder, José Maria Arizmendietta. Even where there is no actual family, therefore, familial styles of teams, close knit and functioning on a consensus basis, often exist at the top. In contrast, of the non-European firms, three (IBM, Sharp and Kao) after a period of family ownership and/or control have now divested family authority to become fully professional, while Microsoft, like Psion, relies on personal rather than family authority.

The Development of Individuals

European labour laws tend to be tougher, at least from the employer's standpoint, than those in the USA, and the role of unions and workers' committees is correspondingly more important, particularly in medium-size enterprises. Many of the companies studied, however, managed to maintain a strong influence over their employees in terms of values and attitudes. Most (Mondragón, Michelin, Trumpf, Salomon, Banco de Santander) had a lifetime employment policy and stressed continuity and development, although some companies had recently had to violate this policy due to general economic conditions. The archetypal approach towards employees is a paternalistic one; values such as leadership, discipline, giving example, work ethics and a craftsman's understanding of the business have to be accepted by everyone. The last word can be left to Trumpf's Chairman, Dr Berthold Leibinger: 'I believe in the necessity of authority in life. My ideal is to be an enlightened patriarch, somebody who is responsible for a task and who knows that he must care for others and who is aware that he is dependent on others.'

The end result is an emphasis on continuity and long-term employment in a profession and a company that is in marked contrast to Japan and the United States. In Japanese companies, human resource policies seek to provide employees with the maximum level of diversified experience, so that 'knowledge crews' can be composed of people from many and varied backgrounds. The usual route is to transfer employees between departments or divisions within the firm every few years. In the USA, diversity of experience is provided by employees themselves, who tend to be more mobile between firms; this mobility is even more pronounced among skilled workers. It is not uncommon for knowledge workers to be hired by a firm to work on a particular project and then to leave the company when that project is finished. European models, however, tend to focus much more on nurturing and maintaining elites over the long-term; not surprisingly, given the long-term focus of many innovation strategies.

There is a strong emphasis on continuity. Japanese firms move their innovators around inside the firm to help them gain experience; in the United States, people move from company to company to acquire skills and experience. In Europe, however, managers responsible for innovation often stay in the same function in the same company, slowly building on their core skills, experience and knowledge. At first sight this appears to be a recipe for stagnation. What keeps these people where they are, and what drives them to continue to innovate? The answers lie in leadership, with leaders who can inspire people to give of their best in the quest for both truth and market advantage; and in structure, in a hierarchy which enables people to innovate, encourages them to take risks and to pursue their own dreams and goals, yet gives them security and stability by defining their roles and their relations with those around them. No nebulous teams, no loosely structured lines of responsibility, but vision and focus; this is what enabling bureaucracy means, and this is why European companies are able to retain talented innovators through the long term.

Separation from the Market

Certainly it can be asked, given the European experience, whether very flat, non-hierarchical organizations do not exchange one form of slavery for another, that of the organization for that of the market. In Chapter 4 it was noted that many European firms remove their R&D teams from close proximity to the market. In some cases, the most extreme of which is Mondragón's Ikerlan co-operative, the R&D function is virtually a separate organization; in others, such as Salomon and Michelin, it is an elite team working very close to top management; in still others, such as Psion and Versace, top managers themselves are the prime innovators. In all these cases, the innovators are much less close to the market, and less susceptible to day-to-day business pressures, than their US and Japanese counterparts. Even in Bertelsmann, where leadership is more devolved, innovation is driven from the centre rather than by market pressures.

The effects of this divergence can be seen in three important areas. First, the innovation focus in European firms is often on the long-term. Salomon's time horizon for innovation, for example, is 'as long as it takes'. First-mover advantage is less important than getting the product right. This is in marked contrast to the time-to-market and market-led approaches of US and Japanese firms; while Japanese firms might try to schedule a new product launch as often as every sixteen months, many European firms are often happy to take years over a single product. The reasoning is that when the product does arrive, it will be so technically and qualitatively superior to its competitors that it will immediately capture market share.

Second, and stemming from the above, the focus in many European firms is more likely to be on breakthrough innovation. Salomon's monocoque ski, Michelin's green radial tyre, Esaote's ultimately unsuccessful attempt to build an artificial pancreas, Trumpf's laser tools, Versace's designs are all attempts to stretch – or even break – the boundaries of previous achievement. And, while the ultimate goal of these innovations is of course market advantage and success, there is a sense too that the innovators are also working for the thrill of pursuing knowledge for its own sake, for what David Potter calls the 'passion of science' and in half-instinctive pursuit of the three great Platonic ideals that have guided European culture almost since its inception.

Third, and stemming from both of these, is the creation of innovation elites, sources of core thought and knowledge on which the firm relies as its well of wisdom. Like bureaucracy, 'elite' has become an almost forbidden word. It is time that it was rehabilitated.

The long-term emphasis is very evident in European companies. The European firms studied seemed prepared to take a very long-term view of innovation; they wait until the product is ready: if it is not ready, the launch is delayed. 'Ninety per cent right and on time' is not a concept with which many of these innovators would agree; time-to-market strategies, popularized first in Japan, are not held in high regard – though are increasingly being used. Nor, by extension, is first-mover advantage necessarily seen as the *sine qua non* of competition; a high-quality product, it is held, will take market share from lower quality products. Salomon are among the most prominent believers in this concept and, so far at least, it has paid off.

In summary, whereas Japanese firms deliberately build the market into the innovation process, European firms often just as deliberately exclude it. Innovators often work in near isolation, not only from the market but even from the rest of the company. Guidance in innovation projects is given direct from leaders (such as George Salomon who said to his engineers, 'Make me a ski', or François Michelin who encouraged his researchers to try a variety of new technologies in search of an ultimately successful formula for a new radial tire). The most obvious example of this is at Mondragón where research and development is carried out by a completely separate co-operative, Ikerlan, which has virtually no direct contact with Mondragón's markets.

Introversion

A common element in several of the European companies studied is a certain introverted character. These companies tended to offer life-long careers to their employees and at the same time avoided hiring from outside to cover medium and top management positions. Several of these companies did not use much consulting help other than for very specific assignments and, to a great extent, organized their own training internally. In this way they prevent their own consciously peculiar corporate culture both from spilling over into the outside world or becoming contaminated by it.

Chapter 11

Trees in the Forest: The Diversity of Europe

In Europe, contrasts stem from the dense and complex European historical heritage. The divisions in Europe following the collapse of the Roman Empire, when the Latin survivors and the incoming Germanic tribes divided most of the continent between them, is a central aspect of Europe. Approaches to managing and organizing, as indeed to most aspects of life and society, differ according to whether they take place in the Latin or in the German areas. In the southern, Latin part of Europe, Romance languages close to Latin are spoken, Roman-type legal systems are in place and the Catholic Church plays an important social role. In the Germanic countries, legal systems are less embracing and detailed and Protestant churches are stronger (Hickson, 1993). Northern countries are characterized by higher levels of universalism, while particularism increases in importance in southern, Latin countries. We will explore these and other cultural dimensions.

Not surprisingly, the firms we studied in five European countries (Britain, France, Germany, Italy and Spain) all showed evidence of national cultural influences. Banco de Santander, for example, was described not so much as typically European but as typically Spanish, with a corporate culture that showed strong values of pride and paternalism. Psion's dual nature, combining both British eccentricity and British conservatism, was seen to capture some of what is typically British. Esaote

Prime Attribute	Rational	Humanistic	Pragmatic	Holistic
Geography	Northern	Southern	Western	Eastern
Form of capitalism	Social	Regional	Personal	Cooperative
Economic organization	Bureaucracy	Community	Individual	Group
Psychological type	Thinking	Feeling	Sensing	Intuiting
Socialization of information	Combining	Socializing	Internalizing	Externalizing
Innovation space institution	Bureaucracy	Clan	Market	Fief

Figure 11.1 Aligning the cultural models

benefited from the Italian institutional environment of public research funding and was able to tap that know-how for its own benefit. Within the context of European-ness described in the previous section, individual firms in different nations exhibit different leadership styles, different types of management structure and different approaches to innovation.

On the other hand, the historical process of innovation in Europe has produced a number of highly divergent and powerful dynamics. Britain remains a world leader in invention; more patents per head of population are registered each year in Britain than in any other country. Germany's engineers, and the education system which produces them, remain the envy of the world. In Italy, the state sector has played a pioneering role in the development of a knowledge base which has in no small measure been responsible for Italy's economic recovery over the last four decades. These are traditions which have had direct economic consequences, and which are part of each nation's core competitive advantage. Ignoring these circumstances risks ignoring part of the foundation of economic success.

On the same theme, when looking at national competitive advantage, it is also necessary to look still further down, down to the level of individual districts and provinces within countries. So dense is European culture that even small countries such as Belgium may have two or more cultural regions; in the five countries in our survey, these intra-national differences could be seen strongly. Just as language dialects in Europe can vary from place to place, so too can cultural differences emerge and disappear again within the space of a few miles.

Examining European business, Alfred Chandler described three main stylized institutional contexts, the Anglo-Saxon, German and Latin areas. The first area belongs to the culture of *personal capitalism*, the second to the culture of *co-operative capitalism* and the third to the culture of *regional capitalism* (Chandler 1990; Boisot 1993). To these we can add the distinctive Scandinavian region, which has not been directly represented in our study but requires attention now; this can be described as *social capitalism*.

Anglo-Saxon Regions: Personal Capitalism

Personal capitalism is a product of the English industrial and imperial inheritance. Early English and Scottish industrial enterprises were usually managed by members of the founder's family, assisted by salaried managers. The archetype of the British firm traditionally included 'gentlemen', the sons of founding fathers, and 'players', the practical men whose ability brought them into partnership with gentlemen. Of course the primary ambition of a player was to become a gentlemen (Coleman, 1973).

The characteristics that are most prominent in English

culture and which are most likely to have a bearing on approaches to management are individualism and the acceptance of inequality (Tayeb, 1988). Individual liberty is considered the most prominent of fundamental rights in Britain, and has traditionally been strongly protected by common law against crown and state. The origins of individualism can be traced back to at least the thirteenth century, by which time the majority of people in England were already 'rampantly individualistic, highly mobile both geographically and socially, economically rational, market oriented and acquisitive, and ego-centred in friendship and social life' (Macfarlane, 1978). The English also assign great importance to class differentiation; family background, education and even accent all serve to indicate one's social class (Tayeb, 1988).

In many respects Psion is a true product of the British personal capitalist philosophy. David Potter, true to Anglo-Saxon 'individualistic form' has been a seminal influence on the creation and development of Psion. Potter is relatively unique in his combination not only of technical and commercial abilities, but also of analytical and intuitive capacities combined with pragmatic and romantic attributes Psion is able to draw upon the tradition of teamwork that forms a strong part of the Anglo-Saxon world, albeit tempered by an individual 'British reserve'. At the same time, the unemotional masculine nature of the interactions within and without Psion restricts the degree of affiliation formed with other people and with other organizations. Whereas technologically and commercially based networking proliferates, particularly between Psion and American or Japanese standard bearers in the high-tech field, any deeper socially or culturally oriented involvement is inhibited. Finally, while Europe is Psion's home ground from a commercial perspective, the company is very weakly networked into European technologically-based public and private enterprise.

Germanic Regions: Co-operative Capitalism

Germany has acquired the symbolic status of the counterpart of the Anglo-Saxon style of management. Whereas 'the Englishman likes to imagine himself at sea, the German is in a forest' (Canetti, 1973). While in Britain firms compete aggressively for market share and profit, in Germany many firms prefer to co-operate. The difference is that between a market philosophy, emphasizing the need for free competition, including hostile take-overs, versus a co-operative philosophy, centred on the concept of co-determination.

The Anglo-Saxon concept of management as a unified profession has not been widely accepted in Germany (Stewart, 1994). In Britain the role of apprenticeship is not widely related to management education, while in Germany the link between in-company training and specialized and general education in *Berufsschulen* (vocational schools) is often seen as the corner stone of Germany's business success.

Germany, together with Japan, has a 'late industrializer' profile, with a rapid (and partly unfinished) transition from feudalism to an industrial society. In both countries, industry has tended to be built on collective concepts of feudal obligations and reciprocity. The education systems of both are more focused on successful technologies and science applied to key sectors; the industrial banking system has a central role and often acts through employers' associations. The governments of both also have a central role through their various ministries in facilitating industrialization and knowledge creation. In this sense the industrial relations systems of Japan and Germany, based on employee participation, lead towards the concept of the 'mutual gains enterprise' in which all share the rewards for success.

The German environment tends to give strong support to cartels and other inter-firm agreements, and fosters commitment to the company rather than providing incentives to sell shares. Merchant banks, insurance companies and employees, through their membership of the supervisory board, are directly involved in the future of the companies. Therefore Germany can be said to be the home of a particular branch of capitalism known as co-operative capitalism (Chandler, 1990).

While it can be observed that, in general terms, German companies have tended to be more product-led than market-led and bank-funded rather than stock-financed, the real essence of innovative co-operative management in the 1990s rests with the so-called *Mittelstand* (Simon, 1992). The *Mittelstand*, or mid-sized firms, have succeeded in entering foreign markets worldwide because they are willing to make strong commitments to the development of people. *Mittelstand* companies expect to achieve the same high standard in both domestic and foreign markets; to this end they do not diversify activities into disparate fields, but focus on those areas where they have product-related core competencies. That is, they follow a strategy that combines technical competence with worldwide marketing and sales, concentrating their resources to ensure superiority in the areas which customers value most.

Bertelsmann can be seen as a good example of a *Mittelstand* company. According to one survey, Bertelsmann is considered to be the most innovative company in the media sector. The core of Bertelsmann's corporate culture is related to the notion of entrepreneurship; entrepreneurs develop their own objectives and have distinct qualities in terms of creativity and responsibility. Employees should be treated as partners (voluntary employee co-determination in the supervisory board). Bertelsmann relies on close co-operation in those areas where it lacks technological knowledge. The decision to acquire or divest a venture usually has not a character of an abstract portfolio decision. Bertelsmann feels that acquiring and managing a company implies taking over responsibility for its long-term success and the well-being of the people employed.

One of the key features of Bertelsmann, and of many companies in the co-operative model, is *intrapreneurship*, defined by Haskins and Williams (1987) as the activities of entrepreneurs inside the corporation who, despite being part of the corporate hierarchy, have been given the freedom to innovate and take risks. Intrapreneurs can be individuals but, importantly, there can also be intrapreneurial teams. Sometimes intrapreneurs are established as outposts beyond the main structure of the organization, but in Bertelsmann they make up its corporate heart. The policy of top-down leadership at Bertelsmann means the intrapreneurs have plenty of guidance as to the lines of business they should follow and the goals they need to achieve; within those confines, managers are free to pursue their own objectives. Bertelsmann can be considered as an example of the particular form of entrepreneurship and co-operation that developed in Germany between and within firms based on a commitment to core capabilities, education and partnership rather than competition in the free market. This has led to what Chandler (1990) calls *co-operative management*.

Business systems in Germany and Japan seem both very similar to each other and very dissimilar to the Anglo-Saxon model. The United Kingdom and the United States were both early industrializers; both have an industry built on middle-class values of individualism and self-interest; there are in both systems clear boundaries between educational institutions and business enterprises, and governments have had at most an adversarial role in business through the presence of strong regulation.

Latin Regions: Regional Capitalism

Italy, France and Spain are in many respects the homelands of *regional capitalism* (Boisot, 1993; Sabel and Piore, 1984). These countries are characterized by strong regional identities which give rise to an innovative entrepreneurship strictly attuned to local cultural and institutional potential. An example in Italy is the Emilian model, based in both central and northeastern Italy, where firms are:

... grouped in specific zones according to their product and give rise to industrial districts in which all firms have a very low degree of vertical integration. Production is concentrated through extensive collaborative subcontracting agreements. Often satellite firms outgrow the spawning firms. Though closely related and highly co-operative the firms remain strictly independent entities. (Brusco, 1982)

As one would expect, a variety of contextual factors – historical, social, legal, ideological, political – support the effective functioning of this specific form of organization. In regional capitalism, organizations survive and develop through being embedded in dense local environments. In one respect the regional environment has a high institutional potential simply because the market becomes a real locally-based social construct. In the Emilian model, the rules of the game give equal weight to family and friendship connections and to economic calculations.

The importance given to highly personal ties between local firms makes the Emilian context much more similar to that of Japan than to its Anglo-Saxon counterpart (Ben-Porath, 1980). In both the Japanese and the Emilian model, successful knowledge-creation processes are widely based in the use of socialization, by which individuals share locally tacit knowledge which is hard to formalize and communicate explicitly (Nonaka, 1991, 1994). In Esaote, the acceptance of a certain degree of regional cultural diversity inside the company between its Genoese and Florentine operations – in regions which possess different histories and traditions – has been a source of strength. The acquisition of the Florentine company Ote led to a transfer of the Emilian model (although Ote is in Tuscany) to the whole company, which is now strongly based on sub-contracting and decentralizing.

In Spain, the embedding of Mondragón in the Basque region is a successful example of the exploitation of the potential inherent in a local region or context in the development of a new organization. Mondragón, a town in a valley in the heart of the Basque country, had a high level of unemployment in the early 1940s. In the area, however, there was an important industrial culture. The Basque country was one of the leading industrial regions of Spain, with an emphasis on heavy industry (steel, shipbuilding, capital goods), but also with a widely diversified industrial base. Father Arizmendiarrieta had in mind a classless society where workers would advance through education and work. Consistent with the Christian concept of man and human dignity, he had a deep trust in the potential of individuals.

Scandinavia: Social Capitalism

Scandinavia possesses a strong business culture which has produced innovative firms such as Asea Brown Boveri and Norsk Hydro. Thanks to the small size of Scandinavian markets, firms in these countries have had to go international even sooner than their southern European rivals, and have adopted many international characteristics. However, core features of Scandinavian culture such as co-operation, commitment to employees, a strong social contract and an excellence in networking and communication remain important in successful Scandinavian companies.

No Scandinavian firms were represented in this study for the reasons described in Chapter 1. However, two examples from published case studies can be provided here, which will hopefully give something of the flavour of Scandinavian social capitalism. The first is Oticon, the Danish company which has established itself as a world leader in hearing care; the second is Norsk Hydro, Norway's largest industrial corporation.

At first glance, Oticon seems characterized by a strong 'northern' rationalism. Procedures and principles are highly systematized; there is a powerful work ethic and a strong product orientation, although Lars Kolind the CEO insists that customer satisfaction must be the ultimate goal. What sets Oticon apart from its rationalist neighbours is its emphasis on people, in particular on human relations and communication. Everything about the firm seems designed to foster good communications; there are no internal walls in the company's headquarters, and at the centre of each floor there is a coffee bar where employees can meet and talk. Kolind believes that learning can take place only among equals and, given the opportunity, people learn instinctively. An atmosphere of openness and dialogue, in his opinion, is what lies at the heart of creativity.

The social contract side of the organization can be seen in Kolind's insistence that his goal is not to maximize profit, but to create value: 'What really drives me is creating value and making about two thousand people happy everyday.' For example, he encourages employees to do voluntary work in their community and supports them in their efforts to do so. There is a strongly intuitive feel to Kolind's leadership style: 'When I make decisions, large and small, the driving motive is what I feel is right, without knowing why.'

Norsk Hydro, originally a hydroelectric utility which has expanded into many diverse fields, has an organization not unlike that of Bertelsmann. The company is divided into four main business units, each of which is characterized by a strong degree of intrapreneurship; for example, each has its own research and development centre. There is also a corporate research centre at Porsgrunn to the south of Oslo, where the majority of corporate research is carried out. It is common for projects to take shape and develop under the corporate umbrella until a result has been reached, at which point they are passed on to the relevant business unit. One such project, OK3, a fish oil product, was developed at the corporate research centre in 1984, and spent six years navigating from one business unit to another in search of a suitable application and production facilities. From 1985 to 1989 the project consumed $25 million in research funds and passed through four separate departments; many companies would have jettisoned long before. However, OK3 had a product champion within Norsk Hydro who was convinced the product had a future, and Norsk Hydro's corporate culture was such that he was allowed to continue. In the end OK3 found a profitable status as a medical product.

These two cases together show several important features of the Scandinavian model. Structures tend to be formal and rational but there is often a strong degree of decentralization coupled with intrapreneurship and networking. At the same time there is a very strong social emphasis on, to repeat Lars Kolind's words, creating value rather than making profits and working in partnership with employees.

To sum up, the character of the European context is related to four kinds of capitalism: personal, co-operative, regional and social capitalism. Personal capitalism, as found in Britain, is based on individualism and acceptance of inequality. Cooperative capitalism is symbolized by the German *Mittelstand* company based on technical core competence, entrepreneurship and inter-organizational alliances. Regional capitalism is dominant in Latin countries and emphasizes regional identities and regional institutional domains. Social capitalism is marked by the networked and decentralized companies of Scandinavia with their strong emphasis on personal freedoms and values and on intrapreneurship.

The Local Level

Intra-national diversity can be observed in nearly every country in Europe. In Italy and Spain this regional diversity is semi-formalized, but in France and Germany as well, regional divergences have their effect on corporate culture. Even in Britain – which has the longest history as a distinct nation – there are cultural differences between England and Scotland, and between the north and south of England; Manchester, for example, has a reputation as a centre with a more co-operative culture with stronger roots in recent business history, while London is seen as having a culture with a stronger emphasis on individuals and competition (Psion, for example, is only loosely embedded in its environment and is focused much more strongly on the character of its founder and CEO).

The corporate culture of Trumpf can be seen as a reflection of the socio-cultural context of Germany's southwest. Manufacturing industries in particular have gained from the socio-cultural conditions in this part of Germany; firms such as Daimler Benz and Porsche grew out of this context, and many technologically-oriented foreign firms such as IBM or Hewlett Packard have invested heavily in this region. Besides these large corporations, the region of Stuttgart is well-known for its large number of flourishing medium-sized manufacturers (such as Trumpf itself). Respect for authority and technical competence as well as infinite politeness are central features of the Trumpf culture which are supported by the broader socio-cultural environment.

Diligence is another element of the Trumpf culture: as one employee put it, 'leaving the company after eight hours of work would give a bad conscience.' Pietistic values such as unselfishness, devotion and eagerness are central, so much so that management feels that variable compensation for proposals and single achievements would be dysfunctional because it could endanger the strong 'taken for granted' elements of Trumpf's culture. There are also echoes of Japan here: indeed we have already mentioned that Trumpf's CEO has a strong affinity to Japanese culture.

Georges Salomon, whose firm is based at Annecy, says that Savoyards like the Swiss have a special liking for well made products, without any defects. The passion for the product is shared at all levels at Salomon. The CEO tests new materials in the ski slopes; on the desk of Bernard Salomon, son of the founder, new prototypes replace quickly old ones. Technical performance needs also powerful design carrying the brand identity of top quality, high performing, beautiful products. Clustered with the other world leaders in the snow sports industry in the Alps, Salomon builds on Savoyard precision craftsmanship.

At Mondragón, paternalism, discipline, long-termism,

loyalty, autonomy and industriousness are strong values of the Basque culture that are respected by the corporation. Mondragón is a comprehensive entity capable to provide a job, an education, an education for the children of the employees, as well as social provisions (health coverage, pensions, loans). The group has spun off its own technical centres that are used by other companies too but can provide fundamental research to Mondragón. The industrial tradition of the region, the generalized acceptance of apprenticeship as the best way to access work, and the social respect for the creative small industrial entrepreneur are values present in the co-operatives that integrate the Mondragón Corporation.

Esaote, with one foot planted in Genoa and the other in the 'Umbrian' culture of Florence, has been described above. Versace also draws on two distinct Italian heritages. The Versace family comes from Calabria, a conservative southern region where the family plays a powerful social role; the firm operates in Milan, one of the world's leading centres of innovation in the fashion industry.

Chapter 12

Complexity and Opportunity: Diversity as a Source of Innovation

Creativity is stimulated by intercourse between communities that are each other's neighbours, but are independent of each other and differ from each other to some extent in their ways of life.

Arnold Toynbee, *Change and Habit*

Culture is a crucial factor in defining the competitive advantage of nations (Porter, 1990). Competing successfully in internationally competitive markets requires that firms match their firm-level advantages to the pattern of comparative advantages within the countries where they are based. Materials and energy, education and training of the work force need to be adapted to national cultures, traditions and aptitudes. In Europe this means especially making use of the legacies of national history, blending the old with the new, the past with the future.

Innovation, as described earlier, is founded on knowledge and vision. Diversity affects both of these areas. Firstly, the pool of knowledge which is available is broadened by diversity. Secondly, the vision to use this knowledge can be more

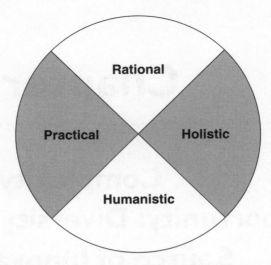

Figure 12.1 Key characteristics of geographical influence

multi-faceted in a climate of diversity, where people with differing experiences and world-views can take the same basic knowledge, interpret it in differing lights and see differing resonances.

These points support why diversity can aid innovation, but it is also possible that diversity can disrupt innovation, simply because the requisite success factors needed to support innovation have not been embedded in the company in a way which respects the company's diverse and unique culture. This complexity of diversity must be overcome before the advantages of diversity can be fully exploited, and the remainder of this chapter discusses this issue.

The Cultural Compass

That the internal success factors need to respect the culture of a company is hardly in doubt. Chapter 7 is full of examples of how the success factors have been modified to fit each of the companies. What is more enlightening and constructive is to build a framework which can help identify which of the success

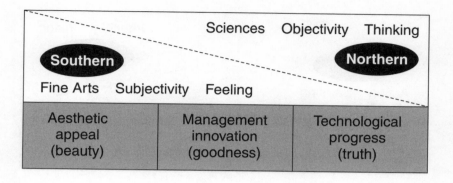

Figure 12.2 Spheres of innovation

factors are most relevant for different company cultures and how these factors might need to be adjusted. We turn to the 'cultural compass'.

Rational 'northern' cultures will emphasise technological vision and industrial enterprise. Technical advances are key goals for innovators who may prize status and reputation equal to or greater than money and influence. Innovation is something that happens in organizations with strong hierarchies designed for this purpose. This is the case in the two German companies in the study, Trumpf and Bertelsmann; it is also true, though to a lesser extent and with moderating humanistic influences, in Scandinavian companies such as Oticon and Norsk Hydro. In Psion, we see a hybrid of the rational and the pragmatic.

Humanistic 'southern' cultures have a founding vision which is based on the organization. Here we see public enterprises playing a major role in innovation, particularly in Italy. The emphasis is strongly on groups, either family groups or assembled teams whose goals are group advancement and group innovation. This strong communitarian feeling has a side effect in that reward systems often emphasise meaning or contribution and consequent status within the group. Esaote exemplifies this model; Versace does as well, though there is

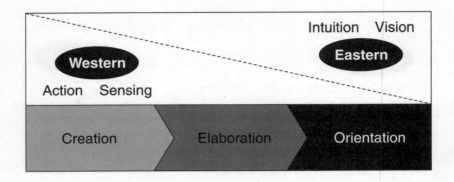

Figure 12.3 Cultural styles and corporate evolution

some holistic influence stemming from the strong family dominance. The Spanish firms, Mondragón and Banco de Santander, also partake of this culture, though there is a stronger rationalist influence in Santander in particular.

Eastern 'holistic' cultures emphasise society and the role of the enterprise in making society a better place. Employees seek personal social advancement as a goal; innovators work to make society a better place. Honour and worth are important rewards. Japanese companies, including Kao and Sharp, typify this culture.

The Cultural Compass and Spheres of Innovation

Figure 12.2 relates the three basic classes of innovation to the northern/southern cultures. Figure 12.3 relates the three basic stages of innovation, or the corporate life-cycle, to the eastern/western cultures.

We do not mean to suggest that companies are uniquely, for example, northern or eastern: an individual company will have a predominant culture but will also, indeed must, contain elements of the other cultures. Nor do we mean to suggest that strength in the specific cultural compass point is essential for success in the related innovation sphere or innovation stage. What we do suggest is that a company must know its cultural make-up, how much 'eastern-ness' it contains, for example, and take advantage of this by bringing this cultural orientation to the foreground when, for the eastern-ness example, it is in the orientation stage, or bring its southern-ness to the foreground when seeking aesthetic innovation.

Chapter 13

- -

Diversity Revisited

Let us pause for a moment to see how the thirteen companies discussed earlier can be described using the levels of geographic diversity described earlier. At the outermost level, of course, there are many similarities between these companies. All are international companies, some of them very large, although it should be noted that the European companies in the sample are somewhat smaller than their American and Japanese counterparts; of the nine European firms, only three, Bertelsmann, Michelin and Mondragón, had turnovers in excess of $1 billion. All have many different national and regional markets and compete, or are beginning to compete, on a global basis. Finally (and this of course was the basis of their selection for the study), all have track records as innovators and have put innovation at the core of their corporate strategies.

Thereafter, differences begin to emerge almost immediately. In the US firms, Microsoft and IBM, we see the power of motivated individuals in the American system. Microsoft has succeeded, at least in part, by promoting a cult of dynamic individualism and encouraging individuals to take responsibility for innovations and products. The competitive atmosphere inside Microsoft is based at least in part on egalitarianism, with conflict and criticism between equals encouraged. Finally the leader (Bill Gates) plays a role which is concerned less with leading innovation than with encouraging it; his tasks include recruiting key personnel, giving them the freedom to come up with their own ideas, and then mediating

159

between their conflicting interests. Gates makes himself accessible to every Microsoft employee via e-mail and promises a fast response to their queries. The result is a flat, flexible, highly internally competitive firm where results are produced in a kind of pressure-cooker atmosphere. In contrast, IBM's problems, at least in the American analysis, seem to have stemmed from its failure to promote this kind of culture. Hierarchy is perceived in America to lead only to hidebound bureaucracy, with the leader unable to establish direct contact with or control over the key innovation processes, which in turn are often separated from the rest of the company. Thus IBM's labs win awards for products which its marketing people seem unable to sell successfully.

In Japan the reverse seems to happen. In Kao and Sharp we see two successful innovators who rely on a strong hierarchy and sense of community. Employees belong, to their team and to their company. The traditional Japanese bottom-up system relies on the development of knowledge within the company, and teams are structured to take advantage of this, but there is no concept of personal 'ownership' of innovations; it is the company that owns them, and the employees are part of the company. This applies to the leaders as well as to the employees; witness Maruta's doctrines of service, of cleanliness health and beauty. The leader is the servant of the company, and of society.

Europeans can with some justice see themselves as standing between the two positions. Here, leaders are strong characters who are unquestionably in control of the company (the fact that many of them own large equity stakes or even majority control, personally or through their families, undoubtedly reinforces this impression). Coupled with the identification of the leader with the firm is the identification of the leader with the innovation process. In keeping with the history of European societies, European firms are often strongly hierarchical; the American vice seems to be a European virtue. But although European firms resemble Japanese firms in this respect, they strongly diverge from them in their structuring of innovation.

Japanese firms develop knowledge from within all parts of the company; European firms tend towards the establishment of innovative 'elites', small teams specifically responsible for innovation only. Paradoxically, these teams are often placed outside the formal structure of the company and are located at or near the top of the firm, in close proximity to the leader.

Moving down a level, within Europe we can see national differences, as noted in the structure of the description above. British individualism, German rationalism, Spanish communitarianism, Italian diversity, French flexibility: these are convenient labels, but they represent real differences in style and approach. And within each country there are also differences. Psion, perhaps, is the least embedded in its local culture, but it is still distinctively a London firm with connections to Cambridge and Oxford: Trumpf is openly Swabian, Salomon likes to point out its Savoyard characteristics, Mondragón is very distinctively Basque, and both Versace and Esaote reflect an amalgam of different regional characteristics. At this level we can see a still further level, that of personal differences in background and attitude beginning to emerge.

Part 3

······································

Implications

Chapter 14

- -

Universal Principles, Diverse Environments, Unique Companies

Do we have to continue to qualify ourselves as a European company, or do we have to lose any relationship with a specific area in order to become truly global?

Carlo Castellano, President of Esaote

The Light and the Shadow

Throughout this book, there has been a primary tension at work. On the one hand, we have the need to recognize diversity and to understand and adapt to the concept that there are many ways to successful innovation. On the other, there is the explicit recognition that there are similarities between innovative firms around the world.

We cannot, it seems, either have one or the other. When we look at similarities, we are immediately forced to begin qualifying them because of the existence of diversity; yet when we carry the analysis of diversity to its logical extreme, as in Chapter 8, patterns of similarity begin to emerge.

This same problem, of course, confronts any writer who attempts to analyse innovation, or indeed business and

165

management in more general terms, on a world-wide basis. The danger comes when we begin to apply value judgements to similarity and diversity, believing one to be good and the other to be bad. It is fashionable at the moment to attempt to explain away diversity or set it aside in order to concentrate on similarities. In this way, it is believed, we can identify generic success factors which can then be used to create a recipe for innovation. Diversity then becomes reduced to the level of an environmental barrier or challenge, and strategies can be devised to overcome it.

The title of this book, *The Light and the Shadow*, was chosen to reflect this dualistic nature of the world. The lesson of this book is that innovation is multi-faceted, complex, capable of taking many different forms in different circumstances.

Business Individuation

The European experience shows that diversity is not just a set of barriers. It can be a powerful source of strength. European businesses have been operating across cultural and national boundaries for centuries, and coping with diversity is part of the European heritage. The interplay of shadow and light between these cultures has given innumerable opportunities for learning; the cultural characteristics of each country and region have all contributed to this knowledge. But this process does not have to result in a loss of identity. European firms do not have to iron out their own distinctive national and local characteristics.

All the European companies studied have very distinctive corporate cultures, which are in turn rooted in the geographical environments where the companies and their leaders have their origins. A high degree of consistency can be observed between the key elements of regional culture and corporate culture, and companies draw strength from the values of the areas where they are established. At Trumpf, for example, corporate values strongly reflect the culture of south-west Germany, while the culture of Mondragón is rooted in that of Basque culture and that of Salomon in the values of Savoy. At the same time, however, there is a common thread running through all these corporate cultures, in that all are oriented towards the goal of innovation.

The most intense example of the power of diversity can probably be seen in Esaote. The physical landscape of north Italy has long been known to painters for its contrasts of light and shadow; *chiaroscuro*, the use of these contrasts, is a long-established artistic term. Esaote has made *chiaroscuro* part of its own institutional life, with collectivist Umbria and entrepreneurial Genoa balanced under a leadership team that includes the entrepreneurial communist Carlo Castellano and the passionate scientist Fabrizio Landi. If ever a company represented more than the sum of its parts, it is this one.

The end result of this experience is business individuality. Businesses, like trees, draw strength from the soil in which they stand, and also from the passing currents of influence, air and light. It may be that some trees cannot grow in some soil; it is hard to imagine a Mondragón flourishing in the United States (though communal businesses such as Oneida did once flourish there). It may be that some business types are only truly suited to certain cultures; that is the lesson of diversity. But equally, no business is immune to global influences; that is the importance of similarity. Requisite diversity, rather than an ideological pursuit of some 'one best way', gives companies the chance to draw on their natural and inherent strengths, rather than chasing the moonbeams cast by foreign cultures. In a world where every potential source of competitive advantage must be seized upon, this one is ignored only at risk of great peril.

As individuals, organizations or societies grow and develop, each needs to advance both internally and externally. Individuation (literally making whole, through the sum of all parts and, in psychological terms, the merging of the conscious and the unconscious) is the key to this process. Starting out in life with a strong parochial bias, each firm must round out geographically and psychologically if it is to evolve. As far as a particular European business is concerned, be it a Michelin or a Bertelsmann, it needs geographically to reach out to America and Japan as well as to 'foreign' parts within Europe. Similarly, psychologically and culturally, each needs to reach into those hitherto repressed sides of its own nature. In that latter respect the comparatively underdeveloped parts of southern and eastern Europe, if given half a chance, may have an important part to play.

In the final analysis, then, a corporate culture is enhanced rather than diminished by its ability to accommodate its shadow, in what we have termed the global businessphere. Starting out from markedly individualistic (Microsoft or Psion) or group oriented (Kao or Sharp), bureaucratic (Michelin or Trumpf) or communally oriented (Mondragón or Esaote) perspectives, each one needs subsequently to round itself out. This requires a process which Jung has termed 'individuation', that is, progressive self-actualization at the levels of individual and group, bureaucracy and community.

Chapter 15

- -

Towards the Future

By doubting, we come to examine, and by examining, so we perceive the truth.

Peter Abelard

There is a concern that Europe is losing its excellence in innovation despite its traditional strength in this field and despite the belief that diversity should somehow aid innovation. We have shown that diversity in knowledge and vision can ultimately strengthen innovation, but that initially diversity of culture must be accounted for when managing the process of innovation. More broadly, we argue that Europe can best recapture its ability to innovate by returning to its core historic strengths: mastery of knowledge and understanding of diversity.

In this important chapter we move forward from the universal principles of innovation laid out in Chapter 8 and the concept of business individuation descibed in Chapter 14, and set forth the additional imperatives on which European companies, and Europe as a whole, need to act.

Willingness to Change

The first imperative is the application of knowledge, this being the act of innovation. Europe needs to learn to recognize its

169

innovative heritage, take pride in it, learn lessons from it and build on it. Given recent history, a reluctance to explore the past is understandable and a desire to homogenize and avoid the diversities and change that have led to so much conflict is perhaps inevitable. However, Europe cannot afford to resist change too willingly and without enough thought.

America has a culture of change and a belief in the future. This manifests itself in the approach to innovation shown by many companies and leaders, but to a large extent it is enabled by the work-force. Life-time employment has rarely been an expectation, indeed there is an understanding that changes in technology or company structure will lead to changes in employment but that other, perhaps better, employment opportunities exist. This removes much of the threat of change and gives the security to accept innovation or to innovate oneself.

Japan also understands regeneration and change and readily accepts new technology. It is helped by its traditional emphasis amongst those most likely to be involved in innovation of life-time, secure employment.

Compared to these two powers Europe risks becoming atrophied. Part of the reason is a reticence to enable and accept change when alternative employment is not secure, and there is not the confidence that another, perhaps better, job can be found. It is time now for Europeans to take the risk of diversity and the risks of the future, to recognize their heritage and to regain their passion for science, learning, innovation and change. Only thus we will be able to face the future.

Knowledge

Before innovation is the generation of primary knowledge, invention. Europe should increase its investments in R&D, both in value and manpower, in order to rebuild its competitive position. At the moment, it is lagging behind. It trails the United States and Japan in vital indicators such as R&D expenditures as percentage of GDP and real growth in R&D

expenditure; it has fewer researchers in the private sector in all its nations combined than do either Japan or the USA. Between 1984 and 1991 expenditure on R&D in Japan shot up by 8.1% and in America by a more modest 3.7%; Europe's increase was only 2.9%. Europe must have more investment in R&D, particularly in R&D personnel such as scientists and engineers, and Europe must develop an attitude to research and innovation, in both the private and public sectors, which gives it strategic priority in its economic thinking and planning. Failure to do so will mean surrendering the initiative still further, as the newly-industrializing economies of Asia increase world-wide competitive pressures. Even worse, given the increasing speed of technological advance, if Europe does not keep up with its competitors, it may fall so far behind that catching up will be impossible.

We have argued that knowledge needs to be related. Trumpf, Mondragón and Bertelsmann have demonstrated their ability to develop a set of linked competencies, through internal development and acquisition. However across Europe as a whole this concept has been pursued less effectively.

America is full of small inventive companies, often little more than a few people pursuing a technical dream and backed by venture capital. They are effective organizations for invention, where the team is the company and the lack of structure helps inventiveness. These companies often lack the ability to commercialize and exploit their product, i.e. to move from invention to innovation, but are bought by larger corporations with the ability to achieve this commercialization. Thus America has the advantages of small companies well suited to invention, whilst the larger companies can pick and choose the competencies to add to their existing ones, avoiding much of the gambling on which inventive paths will be successful.

Japan does not have this approach to building competencies, but its vast networks of inter-linked companies working under broad holding structures allows an element of the American model to be achieved, that is transferring the ownership of inventions or competencies to where they can best contribute.

Overall, spheres of knowledge include technological advancement (truth), management innovation (goodness) and aesthetic appeal (beauty). Again, these phases are not discrete, and all are linked as part of the ultimate ideal of knowledge. Depth of knowledge equates broadly with breakthrough innovation. Breadth of knowledge equates broadly with incremental innovation. Companies should examine what competencies they have, and see if they resonate as a group with the ultimate goal of a multiplied pool of inventions, as a basis for an enriched source of innovation.

Vision

What we have to recognize is that all innovation, everywhere, is driven by vision. Sometimes that vision is simple: a single technological advance or improvement, a new artistic concept, a better way of carrying out a process. Sometimes it is complex: a single breakthrough could create something of both aesthetic and technical significance which has immense social ramifications. The automobile was one such innovation.

However, these visions defy easy categorization. Innovation is, as has been shown, an intensely personal activity, whether it is carried out by individuals, teams or entire organizations. The passion for science (or for art, or for creation in general), alluded to above, is something that comes from within individuals, and no two people will experience this passion in quite the same way. However, the passion will be modified by many external forces. Our culture influences our ideals, through upbringing and education. The organizations we join, work for or even control also have their own characteristics, and this leads to further modification of the vision as we perforce adapt our vision to accommodate others. Culture, psychology, sociology and learning patterns give innovative visions superficial similarities, even as they also continue to emphasize differences.

European companies need to recognize the breadth of activity open to innovation, and that innovation covers more than technology. Their diversity of knowledge and vision can be a source of advantage if they compete on this broader basis, as do some successful companies with a unique 'European' blend of technology, functionality and style.

It is only with a strong vision that the ultimate value of innovation as a path to growth and the future can come to fruition. Companies must commit themselves to innovation, not only for innovating by themselves but welcoming also the innovations of other companies.

Creation, Orientation and Elaboration, Commercialization

Knowledge and vision leads to innovation. But the innovation must be commercially viable and be effectively brought to market. Commercialization is where European companies have lagged, and the reasons are related to the more practical issue of different stages in the corporate life cycle. Strategic goals change and evolve as companies change and evolve. Free from the immediate pressures of the start-up phase, firms are then confronted with establishing themselves in their markets and then, if successful, they need to develop long-term competitive strategies for the future. Time horizons become longer; the innovative vision needed to support strategies becomes more complex.

Further, as organizations become more complex, innovation has to take place on more and different levels through the firm. In the start-up phase, a single gifted creative or innovator may be able to manage the innovation process, perhaps with the assistance of a small team. As the firm and its needs become more complex, the innovation team, its composition and size become more complex, and firms in different cultures adopt different solutions to the problem. Finally, as firms expand into global operations the problem becomes more complex still. Solutions include different and varied roles of leadership, different organizational structures for innovation, and differing responsibilities for innovation within that structure.

Putting the corporate life cycle together with the Platonic model of knowledge gives us some understanding of the diverse internal nature of innovative firms. Time and knowledge separately are important contingencies for any firm; put together, they form a set of critical factors which affect how firms innovate, what their key strengths are and how those strengths are exploited. Here again we see the dualism in action. By breaking down our assumptions about innovation in firms into component elements, we see new patterns beginning to emerge.

European companies, sometimes less sensitive to these issues of management than, for example, American firms, need to take account more of the stages in the corporate life-cycle and re-examine whether their approach to innovation, however appropriate it might have earlier been, is not now in need of change.

Successful commercialization is decisively supported by leadership, elites and hierarchy. These are considered below in more detail.

Diversity and Differentiation

The first and most obvious characteristic of Europe is its history of cultural diversity. Not only does Europe have a strong business culture which is distinct from those of the United States and Japan, but there are even more obvious distinctions between different countries and localities inside Europe. Countries which share borders, Germany and Italy, France and Spain, are linguistically, socially and culturally different. Even within these relatively small countries there are distinctive local cultures; our study looked at localities such as Swabia, Savoy, the Basque country and Tuscany.

All these different cultures have an impact on business, especially on innovation. Different cultures have different concepts and ideals of knowledge and different modes of learning and socializing. However, companies in different cultures can be every bit as successful as innovators; the outstanding records of the thirteen companies in our study demonstrate this. From a cultural and environmental perspective, we can see that there is no one best way to innovation; if there were, then one culture would be superior to the others.

But this point lies at the heart of many of the problems of innovation in Europe. Companies have perhaps forgotten their heritage and applied the generic universal solutions, unadjusted to their unique culture. Diversity becomes a disadvantage when ignored.

But when not ignored, when taken advantage of, diversity becomes a source of strength in knowledge and vision. This must be recognized by European companies.

Companies should beware of generic solutions; too often they exclude much that is valuable. They should be aware of the richness of the global business environment and be able to draw strength from it. Diversity should be seen not as an obstacle but as an advantage. Instead of trying to iron out distinctive local, national and regional characteristics, they should take the best from these and blend them with other models as appropriate. Diversity is only an obstacle when it is ignored.

Globalization today is an accomplished fact; most companies now manage across boundaries. The global business-sphere contains many types of business. Companies must learn their own place within it, and understand the natural strengths which they possess. In the end it is its very own culture which each company has to know and repect, and which may serve as a unique competitive advantage.

Seeing the Shadow

One of the levels of diversity is similarity. It is possible to study, learn from and adapt to the practices of other countries and other cultures; cross-fertilization is not only possible but desirable. There are examples of companies, such as Kao and Rank Xerox, which have deliberately gone out to study companies which were their cultural opposites, learned from them, and brought these lessons into their own companies, all without losing or compromising their own cultural and individual uniqueness.

It has to be recognized and accepted that there are other models besides your own. Where you stand now is in the light; it represents what you aredy know. Try to find your opposite; look into the shadow and learn from what you find there.

Leadership

If innovation is, as was stated earlier, the *sine qua non* of competitive success, then leadership is perhaps the single most critical factor in the innovation process. Where leadership stands in relation to that process, how the leader personally views innovation and the consequent decisions he or she makes are of vital importance. Cultural diversity plays a role here; so too do the practical considerations of corporate life style and personal concepts of knowledge.

As a result we see many different leadership styles for innovation; the negotiator (Bill Gates), the philosopher (Yoshio Maruta), the paternalist (Berthold Leibinger, Emilio Botin) and the hands-on designer (Gianni Versace, David Potter). The need for the leader to provide vision is a constant; what that vision is and how it is interpreted is dependant on many factors. European leaders need to inspire their companies with a passion for innovation: in Part 4 we describe nine behavioural archetypes.

One caveat. Leaders need an organization which must reflect and balance their own strengths. The nature of the organization must be suited to the leader, and vice versa. It is not enough to have a strong organization and a strong leader; the two must be compatible and capable of working in harmony.

Leaders can pass through the three innovation phases: creation, elaboration and orientation. These phases are not discrete; each partakes of the others, but one phase will always be dominant. Nevertheless, in every sphere leaders must both motivate subordinates and channel their efforts. Founding vision is a key global characteristic of innovative companies.

Leadership styles can be said to depend on two sets of characteristics: evolution and dominant spheres of knowledge. At the same time, leaders are also individuals. They are shaped by culture and personal inclination. Their natural tendencies are to manage according to their dominant traits in the business-sphere.

Hierarchy

We found that relatively flat structures and use of teamwork were widespread across successful organizations. However, care needs to be taken.

'Flat structure' has been one of the mantras of recent years, as firms have delayered and reorganized in an attempt to bring the leadership closer to the bottom levels of the organization and improve communications. This in itself has been a good thing; but there has been much inappropriate use of this technique in an effort to get firms to conform to some sort of perceived universal model. In fact, successful innovative firms have had quite different approaches to restructuring.

Usually within the mantra, firms have tried to create structures where control is reduced and where individual employees enjoy more freedom. Internal competition is used to stimulate creativity, with a corresponding loss of security for the employees in these internal markets. Competition within firms can be very successful at stimulating creativity, as at Microsoft; embedding knowledge at all levels of the firm can lead to breadth and depth of innovation, as at Kao and Sharp.

Other firms have reduced the height of their hierarchies, but though the pyramid may remain flatter they are still pyramids. No one, looking at firms such as Trumpf, Banco de Santander, Salomon or Michelin, would regard the leader as being anywhere other than at the absolute apex of the firm. Pyramidal structures provide very strong control, and especially provide opportunities for leaders in the paternalist European tradition to make their own impression on the firm. Further, these hierarchical structures, combined with paternalism, can lead to employees being given greater security. Far from being formal-rationalist and confining, these structures can actually give innovative employees greater freedom to create; knowing that their positions are secure, they can devote more energy to creation and less to securing their own jobs. Though we see the strengths of the first, 'flat' approach, we argue in favour of greater hierarchy and control than is common.

The European tradition is a hierarchical one. Europe offers a variety of structural models from which companies in search of requisite structure can choose. To borrow Weberian terms, hierarchies can be built upon substantive and practical rationality, as well as formal rationality.

Structure gives form and shape, as well as control. Businesses which establish structures need not hesitate to step outside those structures when need demands. Flexibility, not simplicity, is the key. In that sense, bureaucracy can be enabling, not restrictive.

There is nothing innately better about flat, open structures. They are not less complex; they are less formal, and this can actually complicate the managerial task and reduce efficiency. Conversely, there is nothing innately bad about hierarchy. Hierarchy can be a powerful device for attracting requisite elites, the sources of knowledge on which innovation depends. It can help leaders channel innovation efforts.

Elites

Earlier writers on management theory have touched explicitly, if sometimes subconsciously, on the concept of elites. Chandler described management as 'the visible hand' guiding companies, in contrast with (but *not* in opposition to) Adam Smith's invisible hand of the market. Drucker asserted that managers, to all practical purposes, *are* the firm, and used the metaphor of the conductor and the orchestra. Both these metaphors implicitly assume that managers are a group apart, controlling and guiding the destiny of the firm and also closely identified with the firm. Their education, their background, their skills and their outlook all can mark them out as elites.

Attempts made to modify this concept over the years have largely focused on reducing the elite status of managers or groups of managers within the firm, eliminating differences between managers themselves and between managers and workers. In the knowledge-driven industries of the 1990s there is often less justification for such a division; workers are increasingly highly skilled and highly educated, and the boundary between 'work' and 'management' is becoming blurred. In the specific context of innovation, Japanese companies in particular have developed a system of bottom-up innovation which is very powerful, while in the USA Microsoft has been successful through developing an open-access culture where the leader is seen as a moderator rather than a driver.

However, there is an alternative model, one which is much more in keeping with the European tradition of hierarchy and structure. This model involves the deliberate recruitment, development and retention of innovative elites, that is, people who will form a separate team or teams directly responsible to top management and directly responsible for carrying out innovation-related tasks. These men and women are specialists, usually highly educated and usually strongly driven by Potter's 'passion for science'. Japanese knowledge crews are designed specifically to include *breadth* of knowledge, by including people from many different backgrounds; their European counterparts focus more on *depth* of knowledge, recruiting skilled specialists with a range of both practical and theoretical knowledge.

Elites allow a concentration of innovative power. In theory, at least, they allow leaders to bring together a team with extraordinary experience and skills, and with their own private passions for science and art, and then give them the freedom to create. In the European model, these teams work close to the leader and are able to directly interpret the leader's vision for innovation, reporting directly to him and meeting with him sometimes on a daily basis.

The flip side is that, again in theory, by concentrating innovation among elites the firm loses some of its ability to diffuse information and innovation throughout the firm. Microsoft's internal competition and Japanese knowledge works are probably more efficient at this, and looking at the recent history of our European innovators we can see that this is an area where they have been working to make improvements. However, improved communication and diffusion are possible without abandoning the elite concept, and it is this lesson which European firms in particular need to learn.

Elites are the visible hand which shapes the destinies of firms. They must be developed and handled with care. They value both freedom and stability: the freedom in which to create and the stability which allows them to concentrate on creation.

However, elitism should be intellectual, not social. Innovative elites make a powerful contribution, but they must not be entirely separated from the rest of the firm.

There are many models for the creation of elites. The European model stresses long-term development and stability. European innovators are elites by upbringing, inclination and tradition. They tend to be artists, scientists, engineers and scholars. The model of Japan concentrates on breadth of experience within firms, while that of the USA focuses on developing experience by transferring between firms. Each has its own form of truth; none should be ignored.

Wider Roles

For European companies to recapture the opportunity of innovation involves more than simply looking inwards into themselves. Companies need to look outwards and be willing to accept the innovations of others.

Governments also have a role: they must create a business climate in which innovation can thrive. Tax systems should incentivize companies to innovate; regulatory systems should not stifle innovation; legal systems need to recognize traditional concerns whilst not discouraging companies to avoid the risks of the new (an area which America has got wrong to a large extent with its product liability laws); and finally and perhaps most importantly, educational systems need to show leadership in encouraging innovative thought and providing innovators as role models. They must encourage and develop those leaderships and elites, not discourage them as the egalitarian tendencies of some European countries do. By reversing this tendency, and in addition encouraging competition amongst universities on a national and international basis, Europe has the chance to make use of its rich potential of diverse cultures and thus further improve its position in the global competition.

Part 4

·····································

The Leadership of Innovation

Chapter 16

- -

Music, Conductor and Orchestra

Successful innovation ... is a special case of the social phenomenon of leadership.

Joseph Schumpeter

Introduction

Throughout this discussion there has been one constant, a *leitmotif* that has coloured every consideration of innovative firm, whether at the level of global similarity or regional, national or intra-national diversity. That theme is the role of leadership, the powerful catalyst and stimulant which drives innovation and ensures that innovative ideas are translated into reality.

As discussed in Chapter 8, strong leadership is a common feature of all the firms we studied. However, the leaders in question have exhibited very different styles and approaches, not only to innovation but to management in general. Some of those differences can be related to culture and environment; the values of the cultures in which business leaders are born, raised, educated and gain experience are of course a powerful influence on their thinking and attitudes. However, there are other differences which relate to the character of innovation itself, and it is to those differences that we come on the last stage of our journey through the light and the shadow.

The last level of diversity which we need to examine is that of innovation itself. Innovation is of course not a single task. Reference was made in Chapter 4 to its multi-layered and multi-faceted nature, and to the differences between process, product and market innovation, to choose only a few examples. Deeper than these, however, there are fundamental differences in the nature of innovation which reflect the needs of the company and the vision of its leader. We can refer to these as, respectively, *time-contingent innovation*, which reflects the current stage in the corporate life cycle and corresponding corporate needs for creation, orientation and elaboration, and *knowledge-contingent innovation*, which reflects organizational and personal visions and interpretations of the ideals of truth, goodness and beauty.

Time-contingent spheres of innovation are linked, at least to some extent, to the firm's own evolution and its current stage in the corporate life cycle; thus there can be said to be *creation*, *elaboration* and *orientation* spheres. Knowledge-dependent spheres are linked on the kinds of thinking and mental processes required to generate innovation; they can be divided into *technological progress*, *management innovation* and *aesthetic appeal*.

While these different spheres of innovation can be distinguished, however, it would be an error to assume that any particular innovation activity takes place within one sphere alone. The human mind does not work this way. Instead we speak of dominant spheres, in which certain time-contingent and knowledge-contingent themes dominate and others are reduced to secondary importance; but they are never eliminated entirely.

Structuring the spheres of innovation in this way allows us to create a sort of 'map' of the construct of 'knowledge' and the ways in which it is linked to the spheres of social life. Most importantly, it allows us to define different aspects of *innovation-oriented leadership*. By doing so, we can see that there is no single type of innovation, nor is there any one leadership characteristic which is necessary for successful innovation. Instead, there is a constantly shifting mosaic of qualities and attributes, some of which take on greater prominence at certain times but all of which are ultimately necessary for a rounded and holistic vision of leadership for innovation.

The Conductor and the Orchestra: Links Between Innovation and Leadership

The strong interdependence between leadership and innovation has already been amply demonstrated. The core European strengths referred to earlier are obviously dependent on leadership ability, but different leaders have different approaches to innovation: contrast the close personal involvement of Georges Salomon, François Michelin and Gianni Versace, or the leadership from the centre concepts espoused by Mondragón and Bertelsmann, with the egalitarian, bottom-up approaches found in Microsoft or Kao. The need for leadership in some form, however, is a given.

The promotion and facilitation of innovation is perhaps the most difficult of all managerial tasks. Managers are required to be both catalysts and stewards of innovation processes. This means more than just inspiring subordinates to generate novel ideas, for ideas alone do not constitute innovation. The stream of new ideas must be sifted, the valuable ones identified, and assessments made as to whether there is a market opportunity and whether the firm has the resources and competencies to exploit that opportunity. The leadership task is not only about stimulating innovation but also turning that innovation into competitive advantage. IBM's difficulties in the 1980s stemmed in part from its failure in many cases to do the latter.

One of the most popular metaphors for leadership in this

context is often that of a conductor leading an orchestra, who pulls together the efforts of many different musicians and diverse musical instruments so that they follow the same score and play the same tune. However, there are obvious limits to this metaphor, which in the terms of the last chapter is very much a western concept. The idea is that the leader can set the tone for innovation and all the players in the orchestra will do their creative best to follow that tone. In reality, a symphony orchestra is much more complex and hierarchical, and players are required to follow the musical structure laid down by the composer (a much more 'northern' attitude); a trumpet player cannot add a phrase of his or her own devising to a performance of Mozart, no matter how brilliant that phrase may be. In jazz bands (an outgrowth of 'southern' and 'western' cultures) more musical freedom on the part of players is encouraged.

Further, in this metaphor the focus is on one particular piece of music, one particular project. When the piece of music ends, the project is over and the composer and orchestra move on to the next, which may have no real relationship to the piece just played (although the musicians may have acquired new experiences and may have learned to interpret the music in innovative ways). Given the multilevel nature of innovation, metaphors such as this which only concern the pattern of direct face-to-face contact between leaders and their followers (Allport, 1924) with a focus on a particular project, seem to be too narrow. They do not capture all the leadership functions which are of potential relevance in the course of innovation. In particular, especially in the case of larger corporations, it has been shown that leadership by top management makes a significant contribution to a firm's innovativeness, even though top executives are not as a rule involved in personal interactions with all the individuals involved in the innovation process.

We need therefore to apply a broader concept of leadership, such as Stogdill's (1959) classic definition according to which leadership is 'the initiation and maintenance of structure in expectation and interaction'. In order to explain this, let us stay for a moment with music. Music and innovation have much in common. Both are essentially creative; both are about combining diverse elements into a harmonious whole; both have strict structures within which there is great creative possibility. Both are essentially rational. Innovation is bounded by the limits of science and technology, while music is founded on mathematics. In ancient Greece, the mathematician Pythagoras hypothesized that all objects, including the world itself, have their own musical tone; when the University of Paris was founded in the twelfth century, music was taught as an adjunct of mathematics, and medieval scholars perceived music as a celestial manifestation of mathematics, a sound which accompanied the movement of spheres in the galaxy. It is intriguing to note that in European history, times of great advances in science, exploration or thought were accompanied by evolution in musical styles; the Renaissance brought Palestrina and Bach, the Industrial Revolution was accompanied by Mozart and Beethoven, the great age of science in the late nineteenth century brought Wagner and Ravel.

So if music is relative to innovation, what is the analogous role of the leader? It should come as no surprise by this point that there is no one analogous role. Sometimes the leader is indeed a conductor, as when Bill Gates intervenes between his product teams and pulls them together towards their single goal. Sometimes he is the composer, as when Georges Salomon, Gianni Versace and David Potter develop their creative concepts. But what of Carlos Castellano or Haruo Tsuji, who are not personally responsible for innovations? They are neither composers or conductors; their leadership role is not so much creative as part of the act of creation. We can almost compare them to the music itself, a dominant theme or phrase which unifies the rest of the music and both draws the piece together and drives it forward; like the first four notes of Beethoven's Fifth Symphony, an act of genius that is both creative and created.

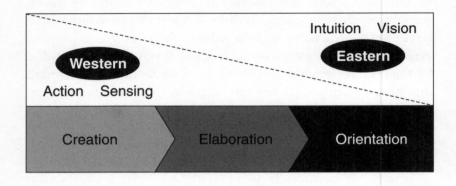

Figure 16.1 Corporate evolution and leadership agendas

Innovation, Leadership and Corporate Life Cycles

Executives committed to innovation and company growth have to manage two leadership agendas simultaneously. They must keep an eye on day-to-day management, getting their people to 'do something'; at the same time they must make these activities meaningful, provide subordinates with a sense of understanding and 'see' promising ways that defy computer logic. In this way leadership can be interpreted as a duality, which involves at one and the same time operating in the present ('western' action) and envisioning, communicating and guiding the way towards a desirable future ('eastern' holism and vision).

These tasks are present at all stages of a company's evolution, but their relative weight changes as the organization itself evolves and grows. The initial stages of business foundation and survival tend to be more action oriented, while later stages call for a relatively greater emphasis on communication and vision. The nature of the relationship between the two can be seen in Figure 16.1, which is a repeat of Figure 12.3 but which we interpret here in a different fashion.

Theories of the evolution of firms (on which there is a wide-ranging literature) postulate that organizational life cycles consist of typical sequences. The literature on corporate evolution suggests that prevalent leadership tasks and the effectiveness of certain leadership practices are tied to the distinct challenges which arise at the different stages of the evolution of firms. As discussed in Chapter 2, the particular dimensions which leaders have to address during the evolution of firms are those of *creation, elaboration* and *orientation*. Figure 16.2 shows how these three dimensions are linked as part of the evolutionary growth of the firm.

Creation through Action-oriented Leadership

Developing products or services that are in some way distinct and unique is a prevailing challenge in competitive environments, and is most difficult and most important in the start-up phase of a business. Leadership plays a key role in mastering this problem and shaping a firm's early development. The top executives of young and small firms have a strong impact on the climate of their organization, frequently dominate decision-making and are pre-eminent in the setting of goals (Kimberly, 1979). Miller and Friesen (1984: 193) even maintain that small firms' innovativeness and pursuit of opportunities 'is so very tied up with the leader's personality, power, and information that almost nothing else seems to count'.

Getting a business started requires leaders who prefer to take immediate responsibility for doing things. Effective leaders of young firms spend most of their time on the relentless pursuit of operating matters rather than on long-term strategic thinking or the communication of visions. As Greiner (1972: 42) notes, 'their physical and mental energies are absorbed entirely in making and selling a new product'. However, this does not mean that vision does not exist; the examples of entrepreneurs such as Thomas Watson or Edwin

Land suggest that successful company founders often are men or women who developed a private vision of the future at an early stage of their career. At Microsoft, Bill Gates, while certainly not a clairvoyant, could 'see' that software would eventually become more important than hardware, and he was among the first to recognize that setting an operating system standard offers the perhaps most powerful strategic lever in the software industry. In the case of Gates, the vision was the spur to personal action, as it was for David Potter and Gianni Versace.

Elaboration through Institutional Leadership

As organizations grow or value activities are performed within an increasingly intricate network of related firms, both the management of operations and the guidance of innovation efforts become more complex. In dealing with this complexity, leaders face the problem that efficient management of operations may have an adverse impact on the ability to innovate, and vice versa. This conflict stems from the fundamental tensions between stability and change, certainty and experimentation, routine and renewal, transactional management and transformational leadership, single-loop and double-loop learning, determinism and discretion.

Given such dilemmas, a new type of leadership is required. As value activities become more complex and firms mature, develop norms, and acquire an identity, the chances of top executives to directly affect organizational outcomes diminish. In this situation, institutional leadership (Van de Ven, 1986) lends itself as an adequate response to the twin demands for efficiency and innovation. The term 'institutional leadership' indicates that individuals with overall responsibility must concern themselves with institutional arrangements; it refers to the various administrative and cultural mechanisms which top management can use to influence behaviours. These typically include both explicit formal rules and implicit informal norms and values, in a way which not only allows for stability and efficiency but also provides a structured space for innovation.

Systematic attention to innovation and support for individual initiatives from top management combine to convey a symbolic meaning which tells people something about the value of innovation (Schein, 1985). At Salomon, the people in charge of new projects report directly to the company's president, Jean-François Gautier; by instituting direct communication links, Gautier got the message across that innovation is important. Gautier has not only introduced a new innovation-oriented organizational structure, but he has also developed and communicated a distinct vision of Salomon's future, stating that Salomon should be recognized as a developer of 'cult products'. Visions like this serve as a powerful tool for maintaining and enhancing creativity and innovativeness.

Orientation through Visionary Strategic Leadership

As organizations grow, they gain opportunities to use their increased resources in new business fields (Bühner, 1990). Such diversification – sometimes referred to as corporate innovation (Yoshihara, 1988) – requires strategic leadership on the part of the top management.

At this stage of the company's evolution, the two key issues concerning innovation are sustaining innovativeness and coping with resistance to diversification-induced change, which can imply a change of the existing order and alter existing power balances (Yoshihara, 1988).

As organizations become more diversified, they often find their business units operating in heterogeneous environments dealing with a broad array of different demands and pressures. These can mean that the organization as a whole lacks overall co-ordination and the opportunity to exploit potential synergy. To combat this problem, top executives need not only to apply new and effective structural arrangements, but also to devote more time to the development and communication of a meaningful vision, in order to mobilize participants and address the emerging problem of fragmentation in advance.

Clear visions offer meaning; they providing orientations to both higher order objectives and action plans. They can lead individuals to experience consciousness at a deeper level, thereby reducing resistance to change and enhancing their intuitive abilities. These in turn can increase creativity which is the very basis of innovation. As organizations grow, vision becomes still more important as a means of integration, orientation and innovation; it can serve as a vehicle for the integration of otherwise isolated, disconnected or even competitive business units. Very often this vision goes beyond the confines of the firm itself; Kao's vision of 'cleanliness, health and beauty', Salomon's desire to build the best ski in the world, Mondragón's collectivist ethos are visions which shape the firm rather than being guided by the firm's needs.

The notion of visionary leadership varies across organizations. Westley (1991) argues that at heart, visionary leaders draw their inspiration from scientific passions or deeply-held moral dispositions. Besides these sources, it seems that aesthetic convictions can play a certain role; this is particularly true in the case of firms such as Versace. These inspirations are closely related to different types of rationality which in turn underlie and shape the content of innovation; by combining these inspirational, knowledge-dependent spheres with the operational, time-dependent spheres described above, we can come closer to understanding the relationship between innovation and leadership.

Typology of Innovation-oriented Leadership Styles

From the above it should be concluded that leadership styles vary according to the dominant focus of innovation. Especially in the start-up phase of a business, leadership practices in firms with a dominant focus on technological progress differ from those which emphasize aesthetic appeal, and the prevailing

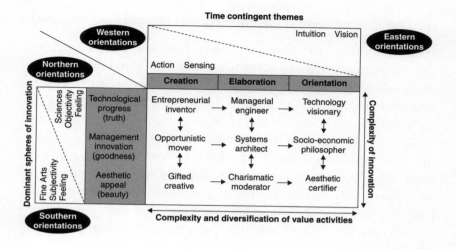

Figure 16.2 Leadership roles

forms of leadership exhibited in these firms are markedly different from leadership behaviours in firms with a focus on management innovation. The two dimensions, evolutionary phase and sphere of knowledge, are inextricably linked. In Plato's original concept of knowledge, they are again two halves of a whole. On the left side, beauty, goodness and truth represent progressively more advanced forms of *knowing*, while creation, elaboration and orientation are progressively more advanced forms of *doing*.

Linking the two halves together, we can see that in each time-contingent sphere the firm may be operating in any of the three knowledge contingent spheres. Thus a firm in the creative stage may be focusing on technological advancement (truth), managerial innovation (goodness) or products with aesthetic appeal (beauty). The range of possible relationships can be found on a two-dimensional matrix leading to nine leadership-archetypes which can be found in the life of firms. These are described briefly below.

1. The Entrepreneurial Inventor (technology–creation)

The technology-oriented, innovative firm is typically founded by an entrepreneurial inventor. Scientific breakthroughs or technological advancements are the most important means to get the company off the ground. In this situation, technological or scientific competence and creativity are the most important skills of these persons and the direction of technology-driven firms is quite often shaped by leaders with a strong research and development background. In the start-up phase of technologically oriented firms, the leadership style tends to be characterized by a strong achievement and task orientation which emphasizes technological progress rather than people or customer needs.

Example
Psion. Charles Davies, responsible for research and development at Psion, recalls the early days of the firm:

> I was the first employee and, for the first few years, we had no formal management system. People worked mainly with the objective of mastering new technologies. It is probably true to say that we have not traditionally placed a great deal of values on interpersonal skills. We tend to take the approach that we can dream up things that the customer will like and do not tend to look to them for new ideas. In the early days this approach was adequately vindicated by sales of our products.

2. The Managerial Engineer (technology–elaboration)

As entrepreneurial inventors become successful in terms of sales, and as their businesses grow it becomes obvious that innovation is not solely the province of technically oriented functions such as R&D; rather, all sources of innovation, external as well as internal, must be tapped. Leaders face the challenge of channelling innovation efforts and taking a more systematic approach towards business.

Example

Psion. Here, as is often the case, the impetus to introduce changes was the result of a sudden crisis rather than the outcome of an proactive approach:

> Our early success had fuelled a sense that we could do no wrong and this led to an ever-increasing number of people who had ideas and thought that we should pursue them. There was no real co-ordination and we ended up with a situation where we began to take on more than we could really cope with. We were soon to face serious challenges to our confidence and courage. In addition to serious technical problems with the machine, it seemed that our dream had turned into a nightmare. The customer didn't seem to like the product; it was not right for the users' needs and it was too expensive. In the end the problems turned out to be insurmountable and we had to start to accept that we had failed on a number of key issues, both technical and organizational.

The managerial engineer takes into account that there is more to sustaining competitive edge than coming out with technological innovations. Since results are essential to survive in capitalistic markets, it becomes necessary to focus more consistently on the market throughout the entire process of technological innovation. It becomes essential to increase effectiveness through the development of functional capabilities beyond that of technical functions. The ability to co-ordinate and control operations becomes a critical element of the leadership function. In short, the perfection and integration of business functions becomes a dominant prerequisite of further growth. While the former requires the firm to bring in people with different talents and professional backgrounds, the latter requires co-operation and the sharing of knowledge among organizational units. David Potter, founder of Psion, puts it this way: 'Unless one group is aligned with the other, you get chaos.'

The creative use of developmental projects can help to accomplish the task of simultaneously structuring and integrating business units while giving employees the latitude to develop their potentials. Development projects can be used as a tool for strengthening the relationship between functions, while still giving employees the room they need to advance their own expertise. It is evident that teamwork is unlikely unless authorities are delegated. Hence, it becomes necessary to move from an autocratic towards a more democratic leadership style. However, managerial engineers still tend to exhibit paternalistic leadership behaviours.

Example

Trumpf. Dr Berthold Leibinger, CEO of the Swabian machine tool manufacturer, is a typical managerial engineer. Paternalism is the essence of his personal leadership concept:

> I believe in the necessity of authority in life. My ideal is to be an enlightened patriarch, somebody who is responsible for a task and who knows that he must care for others and who is aware that he is dependent on others.

3. The Technology Visionary (technology–orientation)

As technology-driven firms grow, the role of the leader gradually changes from a managerial engineer to that of a technology visionary, who integrates business units and enhances inventiveness by virtue of the development and communication of an overarching technological concept which will shape innovative efforts of the company as well as the further evolution of the industry.

Example

Sharp. Atsushi Asadi, vice-president in charge of Sharp's R&D, explains that there is a direct link between such a vision and creativity, and that visionary leadership requires the ability to think in terms of concepts and to see something larger than the face value of an initial idea:

> There is a limit to what comes out spontaneously of a technology. Just trying to bring a certain technology to fruition limits the scope of R&D people's view. Providing a concept in a wider perspective gives them a greater degree of freedom. As soon as you mention such a concept to engineers in deadlock, you will see a gleam in their eyes. All at once their mental fields widen and trigger a series of new ideas. A wider mental field results immediately in greater freedom. Unless you offer them some sort of concept, and not just tell them that they can do whatever they want, they'll end up making just one hit. But if you provide them with an 'umbrella' concept, they'll begin to come up with a series of hits.

Technology visionaries have been prominent in Sharp since its foundation; Tokuji Hayakawa himself can be seen as an exemplar of this type.

4. The Opportunistic Mover (management innovation–creation)

The opportunistic mover achieves entrepreneurial success by focusing on the development of strengths that allow to take advantage of market opportunities. Opportunistic movers in particular exhibit an emphasis on customers' preferences and market trends. They emphasize the fast identification of opportunities and threats as well as the ability to respond to them in time. Also opportunistic movers are often strongly committed to service. Marketing know-how, the ability to motivate and to improvise are the most important qualities of opportunistic movers. A considerable part of what the opportunistic mover does is to use people for their strengths. In contrast to businesses where the primary focus is on technical or aesthetic achievement, strong people-orientation and general leadership skills already play a more important role in the start-up phase of such businesses.

Example
Esaote. The leadership of Carlo Castellano can be taken as a typical example of this type of leadership. Fabrizio Landi, deputy general manager, recalls the days of the company's foundation:

> That's where we started: a circumstance, an idea, a study and some preliminary contacts, where the market factor had a fundamental importance. . . . The cement, the winning card of our development, has been the continuity of the management team. . . . Managerial cohesion has a strategic relevance for success in innovation. People had great importance during the company's life.

5. The Systems Architect (management innovation–elaboration)

In highly competitive and dynamic environments, it is vital to become aware of opportunities as soon as they emerge. Placing a premium on a systematic approach can help to take advantage of these opportunities.

Example
Banco de Santander. The bank tries to take advantage of changes in financial markets to introduce new products ahead of its rivals. A top executive of the bank under Emilio Botin put it this way:

> Innovations are not created in the bank. We have had tremendous successes with 'super-accounts', 'super-funds' and 'super-mortgages'. These products are available in the market, or the conditions in the financial markets make these products available. For example, with the decline of interest rates in Spain you can always take a position at a

low point, hedge it and launch an attractive product. All that is required is to package it, promote it and train the whole network in selling it. Most financial institutions are very slow in doing these things. We at Banco de Santander want to be much faster than anybody to take benefit from the new opportunities in the financial markets'.

The effective systems architect has learned to cultivate variety and to think in terms of systems. Rather than dealing with innovations themselves, the systems architect concentrates on creating a frame in which innovation can flourish. The case of Bertelsmann shows that proper leadership of the system architect allows to pursue innovation, self-governance, and autonomy while at the same time enjoying the advantages of effective co-ordination.

An important part of the systems architect's leadership role is to allow for an organizational environment that is able to empower and maximize a full range of managerial and leadership talents. In order to do so their companies tend to be run as a collection of entrepreneurial businesses. Two challenges must be met in order to allow for the effectiveness of this approach. First, a central task of the systems architect is the development of other leaders. Again to quote the top executive:

> Everybody must innovate; innovation becomes a critical element of the dynamics of the bank, a form of internal competition. Of course, there has to be a certain tolerance for failure if you want to create a learning organization, although 'with the sin you get the punishment'; those who fail repeatedly are sidelined by the organization.

The system architect is concerned about attracting entrepreneurial talents. In order to encourage 'high potentials' he emphasizes the task of acting as a coach who listens, encourages, trains, and provides direction. Second, as explained above, the decentralization of decision-making processes together with the diversification of activities naturally produces various 'centrifugal forces' that tend to diminish corporate integration. The system architect is keen to avoid that decentralization is stretched out to the point where dysfunctional consequences would outweigh the advantages stemming from individual freedom and autonomy.

6. The Socio-economic Philosopher (management innovation–orientation)

Another major element of control is a set of fundamental rules that reflect the leader's beliefs and values. The practices of the systems architect are likely to be complemented by a leadership style which we might label 'socio-economic philosopher'. The latter tries to link corporate activities with social developments in the external environment. The company is conceptualized as a reflection of broader social ideals; at the same time, the company is seen as an instrument that facilitates the realization of values which guide the societal evolution.

Example
Bertelsmann. This type of leadership can be illustrated by the philosophy of Bertelsmann's former chairman Reinhard Mohn:

> People have a different perception of themselves today than in the past. We have helped them to get there: through democracy, through education, through a higher standard of living. . . . The overriding objective of this company is to make a contribution to people's lives and the society. . . . If, for example, we have formulated an internal order, expressed in the form of our corporate constitution, then that is a building block of social policy. . . . If, for example, we say that the personal property of the entrepreneur Mohn or his family be transferred to the Bertelsmann Foundation to a large extent, then why did we do so? . . . We wanted to secure the continuity of capital. And through non-profit projects, systems development and many other activities we

wanted to meet our commitments to society. . . . In the balance sheet of your life the qualitative results will be valued higher than the quantitative ones.

Socio-economic philosophers are common in mature companies where a central guiding vision of the type described above is critical to success. Javier Mongelos and Yoshio Maruta are two other strong exhibitors of this type of leadership.

7. The Gifted Creative (aesthetic–creation)

The gifted creative is very much concerned about the aesthetics of concepts and has typically less regard for market chances. Individuals of this type are mostly found in business fields such as fashion or entertainment. A strong personal taste or aesthetic conviction as well as creativity are the most important qualities of such persons. In the start-up phase of their business they typically work as independent contributors who develop concepts for other companies. In order to satisfy the need for innovative concepts the gifted creative gradually employs other creative persons working under his or her aesthetic guidance.

Examples
Versace and Psion. Of the thirteen leaders studied, Gianni Versace perhaps best exemplifies the gifted creative archetype. However, there are strong gifted creative overtones to David Potter, who describes himself as having a romantic view of science and is strongly influenced by his passion for creation. Though technology and aesthetics are two different concepts, it is worth remembering that in the minds of some, at least, the links between them are very strong.

8. The Charismatic Moderator (aesthetic–elaboration)

A cutting-edge aesthetic creates demand. Given the success of designs or other forms of artistic achievements the gifted creative may decide to internalize a larger share of the value-added, i.e. he or she may embark on exploiting creative concepts himself or herself rather than providing others with the opportunity to do so. This requires a wider range of operations. However, the gifted creative may lack the capital or know-how to adequately correspond to this necessity. The pragmatic solution to this problem is found in the 'quasi-integration' of value activities, such as the establishment of inter-organizational networks of creative, producing and distributing entities. Such partnerships are cooperative relationships where the participants are highly dependent on one another. They may be a useful way to circumvent the aforementioned problems, but they can be confronted with managerial difficulties.

The implication is that there are pressures on the gifted creative to spend a larger proportion of his time on business issues versus using his talent in the area which made the venture successful in the first place. A potential solution to this problem is to assign formal management responsibility to individuals who concentrate on managing the business. The dilemma here is whether to assign these managerial responsibilities to a member of the initial team or to bring in professional managers from outside the firm. The problem with the first solution is that in a business focusing on some sort of aesthetic appeal, few of whom chose this profession are interested in management issues, and there may be no individual with the interest or talent to give up design responsibility for management responsibility. This suggests that perhaps it is more effective to recruit managers from outside who have proven management skills. Of course the problem is that these people will not know the business and, in addition, frequently have a difficult time earning the respect of the creative people and individuals in collaborating firms. One interesting solution to this problem is to bring in family members.

Example

Versace. Gianni Versace brought in his brother Santo as a manager. As a family member Santo had the respect and trust of the creative people and provided his brother Gianni with complete freedom to harness his creative talents. While Santo Versace focused on the co-ordination of operations Gianni Versace through his creative charisma, provided the creative personnel as well as members of the external network with an identity which allowed for 'soft' integration.

9. The Aesthetic Certifier (aesthetic–orientation)

Aesthetic certifiers are those on whom others rely for information about the quality of aesthetic goods (Mossetto, 1993). In order to be identified as an aesthetic certifier it is necessary to become highly visible to the general public.

Examples

Versace, Salomon. Gianni Versace was able to gain a high visibility through fashion shows and the creation of theatre costumes for international artists. In addition he represented Italy in many international exhibitions. Such activities provided him with an opportunity to disseminate his aesthetic philosophy both implicitly and explicitly. In a similar fashion, Salomon has aimed to set standards in product lines such as skis and golf clubs.

To become an aesthetic certifier is not only a matter of prestige; it also provides a company with additional opportunities. As the business of the charismatic moderator becomes more visible and the charismatic person is seen as a reliable judge in questions of aesthetic it becomes a viable option to transfer the aesthetic philosophy underlying the original product range to other classes of products. This ultimately gives rise to a strategy of diversification. Versace, for instance, is now involved in the production of such diverse products as accessories, textiles, watches, jewellery, perfumes and home furniture.

Especially in the case of successful innovation in the field of aesthetics it is obvious that the tasks of leadership and management are fairly different. It even appears that effective leadership of the creative person requires to emphasize the development and communication of concepts and to become not too much involved in management issues. This in turn requires, that the 'visible' leader is backed-up by a trustworthy and competent management team.

Ethical Leadership

From our case studies we believe that there is a close connection between the ability to embark on management innovation and ethical considerations. One could even say that the moral is the dominant source of long-term success in management innovation. The founders and outstanding leaders of those companies which are strong in management innovations also were persons who held strong moral convictions. Liberty, social responsibility and Protestant values were vehemently advocated by Carl Bertelsmann, founder of the Bertelsmann Group, and these values still shape the activities of the company. At the 1994 management congress of the Bertelsmann group, Reinhard Mohn pointed out:

> My great-grandfather, Carl Bertelsmann . . . asked around his small town of Gütersloh: What do people need? Well, they obviously needed materials for education, for learning, school books. And they also needed spiritual orientation. . . . So he became involved as a publisher, to some extent writing his own material. And on that basis he developed very strict principles for his professional ethics. He could not go in for pure profit maximization. . . . No, it was the responsibility for the task performed for the benefit

of society and of the people. . . . Believe me, this guiding idea, this philosophy, has helped the company overcome many difficulties and survive many trials and tribulations. It was always the same attitude throughout the generations that helped them pull through.

Another example from our case studies is Mondragón, founded by the priest José Maria Arizmendiarrieta. Carlo Castellano, president and managing director of Esaote Biomedica, also holds strong social values. Untypically for a successful entrepreneur, he is also a dedicated member of a communist party. It is worth noting that the connection between management innovation and moral convictions also seems to exist in the Japanese context. The former president of the Kao Corporation, Yoshio Maruta, a man who made his company into one of the leading household products makers, explains the Kao management philosophy as follows:

> Our primary purpose is not to increase market share or to beat competitors. It is to serve customers according to the mercy advocated by Queen Srimala, a pious Buddhist in ancient India or truth preached by Buddha.

Conclusions

The distinctions made between the spheres of time and knowledge are not deterministic. Creation, elaboration and orientation are distinct without being separate; vision requires an element of creation, while creation without vision is often dull and lacking in inspiration; technology and aesthetic appeal are related. Similarly, our nine archetypes are not rigid; leaders may progress from one to another, or even be in several spheres simultaneously. Gianni Versace and David Potter were mentioned above several times; in fact, it is possible to assign several spheres to all of the leaders we studied.

The nature of the dominant spheres, the rate at which these

change and the resulting archetypes exhibited by the leader are of course dependent on organizational and market evolution. A variety of internal and external drivers can propel a leader from one sphere to another. Not least among these are the leader's own personality, characteristics, background, education and ideals. The differences between the leadership styles of Bill Gates and Gianni Versace are as much attributable to personal background, growing up in the Pacific Northwest or Calabria, and their personal ideals, a vision of technological truth rather than a vision of aesthetic beauty.

Epilogue

This is not a prescriptive book. It does not set out to describe a new global model for business, or give a recipe for success. It does not offer a single concept on which businesses can focus in order to become more efficient or effective. To do so would be to violate the very principles on which the book is based. We have had enough of idols; the last thing the world needs is another tin god of business busily converting followers to its own true faith.

What we have tried to do is show that the routes to business success are many. There are many business cultures, many types of leadership, many avenues to innovation. Successful companies come in many forms; successful leaders have many faces. This is no more than common sense and experience dictate. The real world of business, outside the classroom and the laboratory and the case study, is full of infinite variety. Indeed, this is one of the things that makes the world of business so challenging and fascinating; if every company were like every other, if every leader led his or her company in exactly the same way, the passion and excitement of business would be gone, replaced by the dull mechanics of process and the bottom line.

This will never happen; and this is why re-engineering is in some respects turning out to be the light that failed. People cannot get passionate over processes; they can over ideas. Innovation is about ideas, about knowledge, about the thrill of the new. Innovation can be pursued for its own sake, for the delight it brings when it is successful; the whole tradition and history of European innovation is based on a kind of hunt, a pursuit through the mists of the unknown in search of the light of knowledge. That is not a new idea; it has been true since Plato's time, if not before.

What the study of diversity teaches us, in the end, is how little we truly know about these immense and powerful organizations we call businesses. We assume, in our offices and boardrooms and workshops – and university seminar rooms and lecture theatres – that we know much, that we are in the light looking outwards. In fact, ours is the darkness. The real light is still somewhere out there, waiting to be discovered. At times it seems to beckon, as a new Big Idea is put forward, and we turn towards these ideas in hopes that at long last we will be able to see. Sometimes, a little light is indeed shed; sometimes, it fails and the shadows then seem thicker than ever.

Is it too much to hope that the next Big Idea will be not one but many? Can we expect to see companies looking to a variety of routes to leadership and innovation, and can we expect to see governments, universities and business schools supporting this trend with frameworks that encourage diversity and personality within business? Perhaps it is; the pull of the universal, generic solution, the one best way, the magic pill that will solve all problems, is strong. But if this book has just one message, it is that the enduring company of the future, strong and innovative, will be both firmly rooted in its own culture and will at the same time be capable of understanding, managing and drawing strength from the diversity of the world of business.

Firms around the world can learn from each other. Innovation, knowledge, skills; these things are universals, and how we approach them can provide valuable lessons for others, just as we ourselves can learn from others. However, and this may be the most important single lesson going into the twenty-first century as communications and information flows improve and the distance between firms continues to shrink, firms can learn from each other without sacrificing their own uniqueness. Kao is no less Japanese because it learned its approach to marketing from Procter & Gamble. To have tried to sacrifice its Japanese-ness in this cause would have been a mistake, just as it would be a mistake now for European firms to try to throw off their European, national and local cultural distinctness in an effort to conform to an American, Japanese or East Asian model.

Europe has its strengths and its weaknesses. The task facing us now is to overcome the weaknesses but without impairing the essential strengths. To do so will require resources, investment, leadership and vision. It is up to us now to find that European vision and return to those European strengths in order to face the global market from a position of strength.

Bibliography

Abelard, Peter (1974) 'The Story of my Misfortunes', in *The Letters of Abelard and Heloise*, trans. Betty Radice, London, Penguin.

Adler, Paul S. and Borys, Bryan (1994) 'Two Types of Bureaucracy: Enabling and Coercive', draft research paper, University of Southern California.

Allport, F. H. (1924) *Social Psychology*, Boston: Houghton-Mifflin.

Bavendamm, D. (1986) *Bertelsmann, Mohn, Seippel. Drei Familien – ein Unternehmen*, München.

Bennis, W and Nanus, B. (1985) *Leaders: The Strategies for Taking Charge*, New York: Harper & Row.

Ben-Porath, Y. (1980) *The F-connections: Families, Friends and Firms and the Organisations of Exchange, Populisation and Development Review*.

Berger, Stefan and Broughton, David (1995) *The Force of Labour: The Western European Labour Movement and the Working Class in the Twentieth Century*, Oxford: Berg.

Bloom, Helen, Calori, Roland and de Woot, Philippe (1994) *Euro Management: A New Style for the Global Market*, London: Kogan Page.

Boisot, Max (1995) *Information Space: A Framework for Learning in Organizations, Institutions and Culture*, London, Routledge.

Braudel, Fernand (1973) *Capitalism and Material Life 1400–1800*, trans. Miriam Kochan, London.

Braudel, Fernand (1993) *A History of Civilizations*, trans. Richard Mayne, London, Penguin.

Bühner, R. (1990) 'Die Bedeutung von Unternehmenszusammenschlüssen im Rahmen einer technologieorientierten Unternehmensstrategie', *Ifo-Studien*, 36(1): 17–40.

Brusco, S. (1988) *Small Firms and Industrial Districts: The Experience of Italy*, in D. Keehle and E. Wever (eds), London: Croom Helm.

Burgelmann, R. A. (1988) 'A Comparative Evolutionary Perspective on Strategy-Making: Advantages and Limitations of the Japanese Approach', in K. Urabe, J. Child and T. Kagono (eds), *Innovation and Management: International Comparisons*, New York/Berlin: Walter de Gruyter, pp. 63–80.

Burns, T. and Stalker, G. (1961) *The Management of Innovation*, London: Tavistock.

Calori, Roland, and de Woot, Philippe (1994) *A European Management Model: Beyond Diversity*, Hemel Hempstead: Prentice Hall.

Cavaleri, Steven and Obloj, Krzysztof (1993) *Management Systems: A Global Perspective*, Belmont CA: Wadsworth.

Chandler, Alfred D. (1962) *Strategy and Structure*, Cambridge: MIT Press.

Chandler, Alfred D. (1977) *The Visible Hand: The Managerial Revolution in American and Business History*, Cambridge, MA: Harvard University Press.

Clark, R. W. (1971) *Einstein: The Life and Times*, New York: World Publishing.

Cohen, W. M. and Levinthal, D. A. (1990) 'Absorptive Capacity: A New Perspective on Learning and Innovation', *Administrative Science Quarterly*, 35(2): 128–152.

Collins, O. and Moore, D. (1970) *The Organization Makers*, New York: Appleton, Century, Crofts.

Cooper, A. C. (1981) 'Strategic Management: New Ventures and Small Business', *Journal of Long Range Planning*, 14(5): 39–45.

Croparizano, R., James, K. and Citera, M. (1993) 'A Goal Hierarchy Model of Personality, Motivation, and Leadership', in L. L. Cummings and B. M. Staw (eds), *Research in Organizational Behaviour*, Greenwich: JAI Press.

Daft, R. L. (1983) *Organizational Theory and Design*, St Paul: West.

Daft, R. L. and Becker, S. (1978) *Innovation in Organization*, New York: Elsevier.

Davenport, Thomas, 'Why Reengineering Failed'.

Einstein, Albert (1990) *Out of My Later Years*, revised edition, New York, Bonanza.

Einstein, Albert (1994) *Ideas and Opinions*, intr. Alan Lightman, New York: The Modem Library.

Fayol, Henri (1949) *General and Industrial Management*, trans C. Storre, London: Pitman.

Fiedler, F. E. (1967) *A Theory of Leadership Effectiveness*, New York: McGraw-Hill.

Filley, A. C. and House, R. J. (1976) *Managerial Process and Organizational Behaviour*, 2nd edn, Glenview: Scott, Foresman.

Frost, P. J. and Egri, C. P. (1991) 'The Political Process of Innovation', in L. L. Cummings and B. M. Staw (eds), *Research in Organizational Behaviour*, 13: 229–295.

Füredi, Frank (1992) *Mythical Past, Elusive Future*, London: Pluto Press.

Galbraith, J. R. and Nathanson, D. A. (1979) 'The Role of Organizational Structure and Process in Strategy Implementation', in D. E, Schendel and C. W. Hofer (eds), *Strategic Management: A New View of Business Policy and Planning*, pp. 249–283, Boston: Little, Brown.

Gatley, S. and Lessem, R. (1995) *Enhancing the Competitive Advantage of Trans-Cultural Businesses*.

Gatley, S., Lessem, R. and Altman, J. (1995) *Comparative Management*, New York: McGraw-Hill.

Gibbons, P. T. (1992) 'Impacts of Organization Evolution on Leadership Roles and Behaviours', *Human Relations*, 45(1): 1–18.

Gomez, P., Hahn, D., Müller-Stewens, G. and Wunderer, R. (eds) (1994) *Unternehmerischer Wandel. Konzepte zur organisatorischen Erneuerung*, Wiesbaden: Gabler.

Govindarajan, V. (1989) 'Implementing Competitive Strategies at the Business Unit Level: Implications of Matching Managers with Strategies', *Strategic Management Journal*, 10(3): 251–269.

Graen, O., Dansereau, F., Jr and Minami, T. (1972) 'Dysfunctional Leadership Styles', *Organizational Behavior and Human Performance*, 7(2): 216–236.

Greiner, L. E. (1972) 'Evolution and Revolution as Organizations Grow', *Harvard Business Review*, 50(4): 37–46.

Griffin, R. W. (1979) 'Task Design Determinants of Effective Leader Behavior', *Academy of Management Review*, 4(2): 215–224.

Hage, J. and Aiken, M. (1970) *Social Change in Complex Organizations*, New York: Random House.

Hambrick, D. C. and Mason, P. A. (1984) 'Upper-Echelons: The Organization as a Reflection of its Top Managers', *Academy of Management Review*, 9(2): 193–206.

Hampden-Turner, Charles (1994) *Corporate Culture*, Piatkus.

Hampden-Turner, Charles and Trompenaars, Fons (1993) *Seven Cultures of Capitalism*, New York: Doubleday.

Handy, C. (1994) *The Empty Raincoat*.

Hersey, P. and Blanchard, K. H. (1982) *Management of Organizaitional Behawor: Utilizing Human Resources*, 4th edn, Englewood Cliffs: Prentice Hall.

Hickson, David S. and Pugh, Derek S. (1993) *Management Worldwide: The Impact of Societal Culture on Organizations Around the Globe*.

Hofstede, G. (1994) *Cultures and Organizations*, New York, McGraw-Hill.

Holton, Robert, S. and Turner, Bryan S. (1989) *Max Weber on Economy and Society*, London: Routledge.

Howell, F. M. and Higgins, C. A. (1990) 'Champions of Technological Innovation', *Administrative Science Quarterly* 35(2): 317–341.

Hunt, S. G., Baliga, B. R. and Peterson, M. F. (1988) 'Strategic Apex Leader Scripts and an Organizational Life Cycle Approach to Leadership and Excellence', *Journal of Management Development*, 7(5): 61-83.

Jacques, Elliot (1990) 'In Praise of Hierarchy', *Harvard Business Review*, January–February, pp. 127–133.

Jarillo, S. C. (1988) 'On Strategic Networks', *Strategic Management Journal*, 9(1): 31–41.

Jung, Carl Gustav (1934) *Archetypes of the Collective Unconcious*, published in M. Fordham, H. Read and G. Adler (eds), *The Collected Works of C. G. Jung*, London, Routledge.

Kagono, T., Nonaka, I., Sakakibara, K. and Okumura, A. (1985) *Strategic versus Evolutionary Management: A US–Japan Comparison of Strategy and Structure*, Amsterdam: North Holland.

Kanter, R. M. (1983) *The Change Master*, New York: Simon and Schuster.

Kanter, R. M. (1988) 'When a Thousand Flowers Bloom: Structural, Colective, and Social Condititions for Innovation in Organization', in L. L. Cummings and B. M. Staw (eds), *Research in Organizational Behavior*, 10: 169–211, Greenwich: JAI Press.

Kets de Vries, M. and Miller, D. (1984) *The Neurotic Organization* an Francisco: Jossey-Bass.

Kimberly, S. R. (1979) 'Issues in the Creation of Organizations: Initiation, Innovation, and Institutionalization', *Academy of Management Journal*, 22(3): 437–457.

Kimberly, S. R. and Miles, R. H. (1980) *The Organizational Life-Cycle*, San Francisco: Jossey-Bass.

Kono, T. (1988) 'Factors Affecting the Creativity in Organizations – An Approach from the Analysis of New Product Development', in K. Urabe, S. Child and T. Kagono (eds), *Innovation and Management: International Comparisons*, pp. 104–144, New York / Berlin: Walter de Gruyter.

Larçon, J.-P. and Reitter, R. (1979) *Structures de Pouvoir et Identité de l'enterprise*, Paris: Nathan.

Lawrence, P. R. and Lorsch, J. W. (1967) *Organizations and Environment*, Chicago: Irwin.

Lessem, R. (1993) *Business as a Learning Community*, New York: McGraw-Hill.

Lessem, R. and Neubauer, F. (1994) *European Management Systems*, New York: McGraw-Hill.

Lessem, R. and Palsule, S. (1997) *Managing in Four Worlds*, Oxford: Blackwell.

Liden, R. G. and Graen, G. (1980) 'Generalizability of the Vertical Dyad Linkage Model of Leadership', *Academy of Management Journal*, 23(3): 451–465.

Macharzina, K. (1995a) 'Interkulturelle Perspektiven einer management- und führungsorientierten Betriebswirtschaftslehre', in R. Wunderer (ed.), *Betriebswirtschaftslehre als Management- und Führungslehre*, 3rd edn, pp. 265–283, Stuttgart: Schäffer-Poeschel.

Macharzina, K. (1995b) *Unternehmensführung*, 2nd edn, Wiesbaden: Gabler.

McLuhan, Marshall (1964) *Understanding Media: The Extensions of Man*, London: Routledge & Kegan Paul.

Maidique, M. A. (1980) 'Entrepreneurs, Champions, and Technological Innovatio', *Sloan Management Review*, 21(2): 59–76.

Mansfield, Edwin (1968) *The Economics of Technological Change*, New York: Norton.

March, J. and Simon, H. (1958) *Organizations*, Chichester: Wiley.

Miles, R. E. and Snow, C. C. (1984) 'Fit, Failure and the Hall of Fame', *California Management Review*, 26(3): 10–28.

Miles, R. P. and Snow, C. C. (1986) 'Organisations: New Concepts for New Forms', *California Management Review*, 28(3): 62-73.

Miller, D. and Friesen, P. H. (1984) *Organizations: A Quantum View*, Englewood Cliffs: Prentice Hall.

Miller, D. and Toulouse, S. (1986) 'Chief Executive Personality and Corporate Strategy and Structure in Small Firms', *Management Science*, 32(11): 1389–1409.

Mintzberg, H. (1984) 'Power and Organization Life Cycles', *Academy of Management Review*, 9(2): 207–224.

Mohn, R. (1986) *Effoig durch Partnerschaft. Eine Unternehmensstrategie für den Menschen*, Berlin.

Mossetto, G. (1993) *Aesthetics and Economics*, Dordrecht: Kluwer.

Nonaka, I. (1991) 'The Knowledge-Creating Company', *Harvard Business Review*, Nov.–Dec.

Nonaka, I. (1994) 'A Dynamic Theory of Organizational Knowledge Creation', *Organization Science*, 5(1).

Nonaka, I. and Takeuchi, H. (1995) *The Knowledge-Creating Company*. New York: Oxford University Press.

Nyström, H. (1979) *Creativity and Innovation*, Chichester: Wiley.

Pappas, Nickolas (1995) *Plato and the Republic*, London: Routledge.

Parker, R. C. (1982) *The Management of Innovation*, Chichester: Wiley.

Parry, S. H. (1973) *The Age of Reconnaissance*, London: Cardinal.

Pelz, D. C. and Andrews, F. M. (1966) *Scientists in Organizations*, Chichester: Wiley.

Pettigrew, A. M. (1988) *The Management of Change*, Oxford: Blackwell.

Piere, M. J. and Babel, C. F. (1984) *The Second Industrial Divide*, New York: Basic Books.

Porter, Michael P. (1990) *The Competitive Advantage of Nations*, London: Macmillan.

Powell, W. W. (1988) 'Neither Market nor Hierarchy: Network Forms of Organization', in L. L. Cummings and B. M. Staw (eds), *Research in Organizational Behavior*, 12: 295–336, Greenwich: JAI Press.

Quinn, S. B. (1978) 'Strategic Change: "Logical Incrementalism"', *Sloan Management Review*, 20(1): 7–21.

Quinn, S. B. (1980) *Strategies for Change: Logical Incrementalism*, Homewood: Irwin.

Quinn, R. E. and K. Cameron (1983) 'Organizational Life Cycles and Shifting Criteria of Effectiveness: Some Preliminary Evidence', *Management Science*, 29(1): 33–51.

Randlesome, Collin (ed.) (1993) *Business Cultures in Europe*, 2nd edn, Oxford: ButterworthHeinemann.

Reitter, R. *et al.* (1991) *Cultures d'enterprises*, Paris: Vuibert.

Rothwell, R. (1977) 'The Characteristics of Successful Innovations and Technically Progressive Firms', *R&D Management*, 7(3): 258–291.

Ritzer, George (1993) *The McDonaldization of Society*, Newbury Park, CA: Pine Forge Press.

Ritzer, George and LeMoyne, T. (1991) 'Hyperrationality: An Extension of Weberian and NeoWeberian Theory', in George Ritzer (ed.), *Metatheorizing in Sociology*, Lexington, MA, Lexington Books.

Roth, K. (1995) 'Managing International Interdependence: CEO Characteristics in a Resource-Based Framework', *Academy of Management Journal*, 38(1): 200–231.

Schein, E. H. (1985) *Organizational Culture and Leadership*, San Francisco: Jossey-Bass.

Scaff, Lawrence A. (1989) *Fleeing the Iron Cage: Culture, Politics and Modernity in the Thought of Max Weber*, Berkeley: UCLA Press.

Scott, B. R. (1973) 'The Industrial State: Old Myths and New Realities', *Harvard Business Review*, 52(2): 133–148.

Scott, S. G. and Bruce, R. A. (1994) 'Determinants of Innovative Behavior: A Path Model of Individual Innovation in the Workplace', *Academy of Management Journal*, 37(3): 580–607.

Senge, P. M. (1990) *The Fifth Discipline*, New York: Doubleday

Smith, Adam (1776) *The Wealth of Nations*, London.

Starbuck, W. H. (1965) 'Organizational Growth and Development', in S. G. March (ed.), *Handbook of Organizations*, pp. 451–533, Chicago: Rand-McNally.

Starbuck, W. H. (1971) *Organizational Growth and Development*, Baltimore: Penguin.

Stogdill, R. M. (1959) *Individual Behavior in Group Achievement*, New York: Oxford University Press.

Taylor, B., Gilinsky, A., Hilmi, A., Hahn, D. and Grab, U. (1990) 'Strategy and Leadership in Growth Companies', *Long Range Planning*, 23(3): 66–75.

Tichy, N. and Ulrich, D. (1984) 'Revitalizing Organizations: The Leadership Role', in S. R. Kimberly and R. F. Quinn (eds), *New Futures: The Challenge of Managing Corporate Transitions*, Homewood: Dow Jones-Irwin.

Thompson, V. (1961) *Modern Organizations*, New York: Knopf.

Thorelli, H. B. (1986) 'Networks: Between Markets and Hierarchies', *Strategic Management Journal*, 7(1): 37–51.

Toynbee, Arnold (1996) *Change and Habit*, Oxford: Oxford University Press.

Trompenaars, F. (1993) *Riding the Waves of Culture*, Economist Books.

Urabe, K. (1988) 'Innovation and the Japanese Management System', in K. Urabe, S. Child and T. Kagono (eds), *Innovation and Management: International Comparisons*, pp. 3–25, New York/Berlin: Walter de Gruyter.

Van de Ven, A. H. (1986) 'Central Problems in the Management of Innovation', *Management Science*, 32(5): 590–607.

Veblen, Thorstein ([1919] 1990) *The Place of Science in Modern Civilization and Other Essays*, New Brunswick, NJ: Transaction Books.

Vroom, V. H. and Yetton, P. W. (1973) *Leadership and Decision-Making*, Pittsburgh: University of Pittsburgh Press.

Wakasugi, R. (1994) 'Organizational Structure and Behavior in Research and Development', in K. Imai and R. Komiya (eds), *Business Enterprise in Japan: Views of Leading Japanese Economists*, pp. 159–177, Cambridge, MA: MIT Press.

Weber, Max (1930) *The Protestant Ethic and the Spirit of Capitalism*, trans. Talcott Parsons, London: George Allen and Unwin.

Weber, Max (1964) *The Theory of Social and Economic Organization*, trans. A. M. Henderson and Talcott Parsons, New York: The Free Press.

Westley, F. and Mintzberg, H. (1988) 'Profiles of Strategic Vision', in S. Conger and R. Kanungo (eds), *Charismatic Leadership: The Elusive Factor in Organizational Effectiveness*, San Francisco: Jossey-Bass, pp. 161–212.

Westley, F. (1991) 'Bob Geldof and Live Aid: The Affective Side of Global Social Innovation', *Human Relations*, 44(10): 1011–1036.

Whitley, Richard (ed.) (1992) *European Business Systems: Firms and Markets in their National Contexts*, London: Sage.

Yoshihara, H. (1988) 'Dynamic Synergy and Top Management Leadership: Strategic Innovation in Japanese Companies', in K. Urabe, S. Child and T. Kagono (eds), *Innovation and Management: International Comparisons*, pp. 47–62, New York/Berlin: Walter de Gruyter.

Index

Abelard, Peter 4–5, 31
acquisitions 84–5, 94–5
Allport, F.H. 188
American model 14, 17, 40, 97,
    100, 121, 122–5, 132–3, 135,
    159–60, 173, 180
  achievement 123
  egalitarianism 124
  entrepreneurship 125
  individual rewards 124
  ingenuity 123–4
  perfectibilism 122–3
  as pragmatic 125
  self-reliance 124
'and thinking' 19
Aristotle 4
Arizmendiarreta, José Maria 69,
    70, 132, 134, 147, 207
Asadi, Atsushi 198

Banco de Santander 20, 72, 91, 93,
    108, 139, 156, 200–1
Bata, Tomas 21
Ben-Porath, Y. 146
Bertelsmann 20, 37, 38, 82, 84–5,
    89, 93–4, 101, 106, 107, 133,
    134, 136, 144–5, 155, 159, 201,
    202–3
  enterprise, responsibility and
    partnership 62–4
Bertelsmann, Carl 37, 63, 206
Blizzard 85
Bloom, H. *et al* 128
Boisot, M. 145
Bond, 114
Botin, Emilio 72, 177
boundaries 119–21
Bridgestone 64

Brusco, S. 146
Bühner, R. 193

Caja Laboral Popular Bank 70
Calori, R. and de Woot, P. 14,
    128–9, 131
Canetti, 143
Castellano, Carlo 73, 75, 86, 99,
    133, 166, 189, 200, 207
Cavaleri, S. and Obló, K. 114
Chandler, Alfred 12–13, 140, 144,
    145, 179
changing the rules of the game 96
Child, 114
co-operatives 69–72, 95, 143–5, 149
Cohen, W.M. and Levinthal, D.A.
    33
Coleman, 141
commercialization 80
communitarianism 73, 155–6, 160,
    161
competitive advantage 96–7, 141,
    153
Condorcet, Marquis de 122
Cook, Paul 90
corporate
  culture 19
    co-operative capitalism 143–5
    homogenized 13, 120
    introversion 138
    mobilization from the top 65–7
    personal capitalism 141–2
    regional capitalism 145–7
    social capitalism 147–9
  life cycle 29–30, 174–5, 191
    creation 37, 74–5, 191–2
    elaboration 37, 75–6, 192–3
    orientation 37–8, 193–4

see also organizations
cult products 67–9, 95, 96, 101, 193
cultural compass 154–7
  holistic eastern 156
  humanistic southern 155–6
  rational northern 155
culture 40, 113–14, 118–19, 153

Davies, Charles 51, 196
De Geus, 41
decentralization 85, 89, 93, 149
Dias, Bartolomeu 5
diversity 161, 165, 175–6, 210
  European model 14–17
  formalized 119
  future of 120
  geographical 117–18
  global 117
  intra-national 118, 149–51
  national 118
  regional 117–18, 121
  managing 12, 73–7
  practical 119
  substantive 119
  theoretical 119
  universal approach 11–13
Dolomite 85
Drucker, P. 13, 179
Du Pont 33

Eannes, Gil 6
economics 6–9, 38, 179
EFER 21
Einstein, Albert 31
elites 161, 179–81
Emilian model 145–6
employment 15–16, 65, 91, 135, 138
equifinality 108–9
Esaote Biomedica 20, 73–4, 85, 86,
    90, 108, 118, 119, 134, 137,
    139–40, 146, 151, 155, 161,
    166, 200, 207
  creation, orientation and
    elaboration 74–6
Europe, central and eastern 21
European model 13, 14–17, 91,
    94–5, 97–105, 122, 128–9, 133,
    135, 160, 165–7, 172, 180, 211
  Anglo-Saxon regions 141–2
  Germanic regions 143–5
  as intellectual 125
  internal negotiation 129
  Latin regions 145–7
  less formal systems of
    management 131–2
  managing between extremes 130
  managing international
    diversity 129–30
  orientation towards people 129
  strong product orientation 130–1

Friedman, M. 17
Frost, P.J. and Egri, C.P. 28
Füredi, F. 37

Gama, Vasco da 5
Gates, Bill 37, 41, 44, 46, 47, 86, 88,
    93, 125, 133, 159–60, 177, 192,
    208
Gaultier, Jean-François 68, 193
global businessphere 19
globalization 120, 176
Goodyear 64
Greiner, L.E. 191

Haas Laser 84, 96
Hadrian, Emperor 40
Hampden-Turner, C. and
    Trompenaars, F. 114, 121,
    131–2
Harris, 115
Haskins, and Williams 144
Hayakawa, Tokuji 41, 58, 59, 126,
    199
Hayek, F. 17
Henry of Portugal, Prince 5, 6
Hewlett-Packard 91
Hickson, D.S. 139
  and Pugh, D.S. 114
Hofstede, G. 113
human resource management
    106–7

IBM 20, 159, 160
  as innovator *48*
  rise and fall 46–8
Ikerlan 136, 138
individualism 133, 141–2, 159–60,
      161, 166
  development of 134–6
innovation 153, 210
  aesthetic 34–5, 203–6
    creation 203
    elaboration 203–5
    orientation 205–6
  breakthrough 137
  and corporate culture 65–7
  fostering 50
  historical process 140
  imperatives 40–1
    commercialization 32–4, 174–5
    diversity 175–6
    elites 137, 179–81
    hierarchy 178–9
    hierarchy of 89, 103
    knowledge 171–2, 186, 187–9
    leadership 177–8
    vision 173–4
    wider roles 181–2
    willingness to change 170–1
  long-term 136–7
  management 35
    creation 199–200
    elaboration 200–2
    orientation 202–3
  market-driven 32, 186
  multi-faceted/multilevel 33, 38,
      186, 188
  Platonic 34–6
  push/pull 33, 37
  technological 32, 35
    creation 196
    elaboration 196–8
    orientation 198–9
  and time 36–8, 137, 186
  tradition 3–9
  types of 31–2
  understanding 114
intrapreneurship 144–5, 149
invention 33

Ito, Eizo 55–6

Japanese model 14, 17, 40, 91, 97,
      98–9, 100–1, 102, 121, 125–8, 135,
      160–1, 180, 211
  as incremental experimentation
      125
  paternalism 127
Johnson & Johnson 106

kaizen 90
Kanter, R.M. 28, 131
Kao Corporation 20, 38, 54, 81, 91,
      97, 104, 105, 109, 127, 133,
      156, 176, 177, 194, 207, 211
  importance of R&D and
      marketing 56–8
  service, truth, equality in 54–6,
      57
Kimberly, S.R. 191
Klingel, Hans 62, 87
knowledge 3–4, 79, 153, 171–3,
      186, 207, 210
  application 170–1
  breadth and depth 172, 180
  modifiers 29–30
  Platonic 25–7, 195
  resonance 28–9
  society 58, 59
  sources 27–8
Kogut, 114
Kolind, Lars 147–8

Landi, Fabrizio 133, 166, 200
language 115–16
leadership 177–8, 185–6
  action-oriented 191–2
  archetypes 207
    aesthetic certifier 205–6
    charismatic moderator 203–5
    entrepreneurial inventor 196
    gifted creative 203
    managerial engineer 196–8
    opportunistic mover 199–200
    socio-economic   philosopher
      202–3
    systems architect 200–2

technology visionary 198–9
dualism 190–1
ethical 206–7
from the centre 132–3
and innovation 187–9
institutional 192–3
top-down 145
typology 194–5
visionary strategic 193–4
Legrand, Maurice 96
Leibinger, Berthold 60–3, 86, 87,
  133, 135, 177, 198

3M 91
Macfarlane, 142
McLuhan, M. 12
Malthus, T. 122–3
management 35, 199–203
  scientific 14, 131, 133
Mansfield, E. 33
marketing 56–8, 199
Maruta, Yoshio 28, 54–8, 160, 177,
  203, 207
Merle, Carole 99
Michelin 20, 35–6, 38, 64, 90, 93,
  96, 101, 105, 106, 109, 136,
  137, 159
  family-based 64–5
  strong corporate culture 65–7
Michelin, François 64–6, 87, 93, 96,
  97, 98, 104, 106–7, 133, 187
Microsoft 20, 32, 37, 44, 83, 86, 88,
  93, 100, 102, 104, 106, 159–60,
  177, 180, 192
  competitiveness 45, 46
  informality, creativity and
    tension in 45, 47
  personal responsibility 45–6
Mill, J.S. 7
Miller, D. and Friesen, P.H. 191
Mittelstand 144
Mohn, Reinhard 62, 63, 206
Mondragón Group 20, 38, 69, 81,
  82–3, 84, 89, 93, 95, 101, 105,
  118, 132, 136, 138, 151, 156,
  159, 161, 166, 194, 207

blending old with new 73
continuous education and
  development 69–70
independence and
  interdependence 70–2
Project Guide 97
Mongelos, Javier 87, 203
Mossetto, G. 205

Nagase, Tomio 54
networking 142, 149
Ng, *et al* 114
Nissan, Primera project 102
Nonaka, I. 146
  and Takeuchi, H. 98
Norsk Hydro 34, 147, 148–9, 155

Ohgawara, Takaji 58–9
one best way 12, 13, 14–15, 108,
  167, 175–6
organizations 7–9
  bio-functional 56–8
  case studies 20–1
  family ownership 64–5, 67,
    133–4, 160
  hierarchy
    flat structures 82–3, 89, 99–101,
      102–3, 178–9
    teamwork 51, 55, 58, 81, 88,
      101–5, 177
  horizontal/vertical functions
    94–5
  hypertext 93
  paternalistic 61–2, 127, 135, 151,
    177
  see also corporate culture and
    life cycle
Ote Biomedica 74, 75, 85, 146
Oticon 147–8, 155

perfectibilism 122–3
Peters, T. 131
  and Waterman, R.H. 48
place 29
Plato 3–4, 25–7, 31, 174, 195
Porter, M.P. 32, 41, 114, 153

Potter, David 37, 49–50, 51, 53, 86, 87, 89, 92, 100, 103, 137, 142, 177, 189, 192, 197, 203, 207
Procter and Gamble (P&G) 56, 59, 94, 211
product/process innovation 32, 66, 94, 186
Psion 20, 32, 37, 49, 54, 81, 86, 89, 92, 103, 108, 133, 134, 136, 139, 142, 149–50, 161, 196, 196–7, 203
  balancing freedom and order 51–2
  as European 52–4
  fostering innovation 49–50
  remaining independently minded 50–1
  stimulating aggressive teamwork 51

R&D 16, 38, 56–8, 81, 83, 86, 90, 96, 101, 104–5, 171–2
  in co-operatives 71
  origin-oriented 57
  separation from the market 136–8
Raychem 90
re-engineering 14, 209
Redding, 114
Reich, 122, 123
Rhone Poulenc 85
Ritzer, G. 131
Rossignol 105
Rothwell, 33

Sabel, and Piore, 145
St Anselm 4
Salomon 20, 38, 67–9, 83, 85, 86, 90, 92–3, 96, 99, 101, 105, 136–8, 161, 166, 193, 194, 205
Salomon, Georges 41, 86, 96, 99, 101, 138, 150, 187, 189
Scandinavia 21, 147–9
Schein, E.H. 193
science 39–40, 180
Sharp 20, 38, 49, 54, 58–9, 81, 91,

93, 98, 100, 104, 126, 133, 156, 177, 199
similarity 114–17, 165, 167, 176
  fallacy of halves 117
  realist fallacy 117
Simon, 144
Smith, A. 6–7, 9, 179
Spain 146–7
Stewart, 143
Stogdill, R.M. 188
success factors 43–4, 116, 154–5, 209
  blending old and new values 73
  competition 45, 46, 178
  creativity 47, 68, 178
  education and training 65, 69–70
  freedom and order 27, 52–3
  independence 50–1
  knowledge 56–7, 58–9
  personal responsibility 45–6, 62–3
  rationality, precision and accuracy 60–4
  service 54–9
  teamwork 51
  technological prowess 48
  see also universal approach, principles

Tayeb, 142
Taylorism 131
teamwork 51, 133, 142, 161, 178, 180
technology 32, 35–6, 192–9, 207
time
  corporate life cycle 29–30, 36–8, 186, 207
  to market 73, 93
Tokiwa, Fumikazu 55, 57
Toynbee, A. 153
Trumpf 20, 37, 60, 82, 84, 86, 89, 92, 94, 96, 101, 105, 107–9, 134, 137, 150, 155, 161, 167, 198
  competence, Technik, and paternalism 61–2

diligence, engineering and
politeness 60–1
Optimization Program (TOP) 92
Trumpf, Christian 60
Tsuji, Haruo 189

universal approach 210–11
focus on the known 12–13
harmonized system 13, 27
one best way 12, 13, 14–15
principles 43–4
commitment 90–1, 98
competence 83–5, 87, 144, 173
family ownership 133–4
flat structures 82–3, 89, 100–3,
102–3, 178–9
incentives 106–7
individualism 133, 134–6, 141–2,
159–60, 161, 167
information/communication 55,
56, 58–9, 81–3, 98–9, 180–1, 210
leadership 85–9, 132–3
market awareness 98–100
regeneration 95–8

resources 105
strategy 91–5
teamwork 51, 55, 58, 81, 88, 101–5
see also success factors

Van de Ven, 28, 192
Versace, Donatella 76
Versace, Gianni 41, 76–7, 86, 100,
177, 187, 189, 192, 203, 205,
207, 208
Gianni Versace SpA 20, 32, 35,
76–7, 86, 89, 90, 133, 137, 151,
155–6, 161, 194, 203, 205
vision 79–80, 153–4, 170, 173–4,
207

Watson, Thomas J. (and son) 47, 48
Weber, M. 7, 131
Westley, F. 194
Whitley, R. 14, 114
William of Champeaux 4

Yoshihara, H. 193